MEMORIES AND F

MW00612483

BOOK TWO

FAILING MEMORY

MEMORIES AND FORGETFULNESS

Book Two
Failing Memory

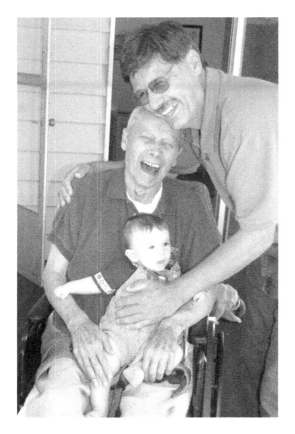

Cover Picture:
Travis and
Bernie with me Circa 2008

By Larry Calkins

FAILING MEMORY

Book Two of
MEMORIES AND FORGETFULNESS

ISBN: 978-1-7344718-4-7

Published by:

Larry Calkins

Copyright © 2022 Larry Calkins

All rights reserved.

NO PART OF THIS BOOK MAY BE REPODUCED IN ANY FORM, BY PHOTOCOPYING OR BY ANY ELECTRONIC OR MECHANICAL MEANS, INCLUDING INFORMATION STORGE OR RETRIEVAL SYSTEMS, WITHOUT PERMISSION IN WRITING FROM THE COPYRIGHT OWNER/AUTHOR

This book is dedicated to:

My wife and children

Acknowledgement

I would like to thank Yuvonne C. Brooks, Ed.D. for reviewing, editing and mentoring me through the writing of this book. She has provided me with insight and responsible guidance in the development of this material. I appreciate her encouragement and wisdom as well as hearing about her life experiences, writings, educational pursuits and teaching young minds. Most of all, I appreciate the fun we had talking, commiserating and laughing together as we worked diligently to address our mission.

Larry Calkins

FAILING MEMORY

CONTENTS　　　　　　　　PAGE

Larry Calkins

PROLOGUE

My father, Travis wrote letters most of his life. He penned many of them to my Aunt Sarah, his sister, around the time of my grandmother's (Margaret) dementia and passing. Dad continued to write letters when he was first diagnosed with dementia and throughout his illness. Eventually, he could no longer write letters to my Aunt Sarah but he left a wonderful legacy of his words which inspired this story.

Book One, Letters From Travis (published separately), provides some of those accounts. It is the backstory to Book Two: Failing Memory. The correspondence chronicles both Dad and Aunt Sarah's coping with their mother's tragic illness. Also, he describes some of his day to day activities to Aunt Sarah by telling of his adventures. The writings display my father's personality, his worries, fears, joys and ambitions. Aunt Sarah and he continue with their letters after my grandmother's death in 1993. Then, Dad begins to explain his own forgetfulness to Aunt Sarah at the start of his dementia.

Each letter provides the reader with a glimpse into their lives, family and associates. My hope is that these letters will involve the reader in Aunt Sarah's and Dad's experiences.

When Dad understood he had the same disease as his mother, he told me, "Larry, use it or lose it." He said, "I kept writing to Sarah so I wouldn't lose my ability to write or to communicate." In 1997-98, he became a prolific writer. Aunt Sarah listened as well as responded in kind which strengthened their relationship.

***

Book Two, Failing Memory (this publication), tells my father's story after he was diagnosed with dementia. It includes my experiences with him and how I coped with his illness. Throughout the time, Dad was ill, I learned more about myself and what I might expect or even want from life. I describe my emotional involvement as Dad struggled with dementia and I with my grief.

FAILING MEMORY

When I fully comprehended the magnitude of my father's dementia, it hit me like "a ton of bricks." After accepting the fact that he had the disease, I was not sure how to help him cope through the illness. I made mistakes. However, I tried to remain positive, provide him the assurances he needed, create circumstances for his enjoyment and offer him compassion as we both traveled through the remainder of his life.

Sadie, my cousin and Aunt Sarah's daughter, recounted the time she visited my father in the nursing home. Dad had developed significant dementia. At the time, she asked me, "Does your father remember you when you visit with him." I told her, "It doesn't matter to me whether he did or did not." I continued, "What matters to me is that he is in a safe place, he has choices about his surroundings and that he knows I love him. I am certain he knows I love him!"

Starting in 2009 and for an additional three years, Sadie told me that those comments stuck with her as she took care of her mother when she developed dementia like her mother's mother and mother's brother before her.

Larry Calkins

***

Unfortunately, Alzheimer's or dementia provides a difficult experience for the patient. For those of us who care and nourish relatives or friends, it offers little comfort. The disease is hard on everyone who observes the individuals who are afflicted. It is difficult to witness the deterioration of a person's mental and physical capabilities.

As Dad and I traveled on the road of dementia, I gained new respect for caregivers as I watched them attend to the needs of my grandmother and father. They woke patients, bathed, dressed, made meals, fed them and cleaned the rooms. Often, they had to lift patients in and out of wheelchairs or beds. These workers deserve our admiration and respect.

MEMORIES AND FORGETFULNESS

BOOK 2
FAILING MEMORY

circa 1999 Travis and Lucia

Lake Forest Park

circa 2002 Dad, Mother and me

Bend\

circa 2002 Dad Bend

circa 2007 Dad and Me

Larry Calkins

CHAPTER 11 – DEMENTIA -THE START
(MY OBSERVATIONS)

In 1994, Carrie and I lived in eastern Oregon. On a spring weekend, we left for the Seattle area to celebrate her sibling's (one sister and two brothers who were all born in the month of April) birthdays. After being married for nearly 22 years, we could travel with less restrictions because our oldest child, Hettie, skipped off to college creating space for us and Marcella was a senior in High School. Emma was also at home. To escape from the day to day drudgery, we journeyed to Seattle because we could visit our families of origin and have free room and board. Carrie and I felt comfortable there. Our families accepted us unconditionally.

During that weekend, I visited my parents and "carried on" a conversation with my father. He described his approach to teaching and life. Previously, Dad had volunteered to tutor students at a local high school and he felt good about his ability to reach young people again. He was well liked. Dad put on his educator's hat and asked pertinent questions of the young person to guide them to the proper answer.

When I was growing up, he practiced with me, so I knew his approach. He enjoyed tapping into the minds of young people and guiding them to a final answer of a puzzle they were trying to solve. This was called the Socratic Method and he created dialog between students to draw out the conclusion. He would ask, "What do you think the answer is?" When the pupil answered, Dad responded with a question that challenged or refuted the answer. He felt the young person would learn much more and retain information if they figured it out themselves.

Tactfully, asking questions worked better than providing rote answers. When Dad used his method to teach me, I felt good about myself because in the end, I had solved a problem. Dad worked hard to perfect this technique. He never made me feel stupid and was not demeaning. His conversational approach appealed to me as he guided me to the correct answer.

Also, he suggested that writing letters kept the mind alive and talked about writing letters to Aunt Sarah. At least once per month and often weekly, he wrote his sister letters, discussing issues of the day or simply what the week had been like for him. Writing helped him keep mentally alert and in touch with people. He encouraged me to write too. Being lazy, I did not see the value of doing what he suggested. I kept myself busy with work and "life on the job," as well as raising a growing family. I preferred to talk on the phone to family members, email short notes or simply visit relatives. I think that's why I liked coming to the Seattle area. Writing seemed "old school" and time consuming. At that time, seeing family face to face appeared to be more important. I viewed myself operating in the age of computers and Dad functioned in the age of typewriters and cursive writing.

Although, I did not listen, Dad tried to explain how writing required the author to contemplate the topic and then revise it to convey the exact meaning. This brain exercise generated critical thinking by connecting the emotional with the cognitive parts of the brain. Writing took discipline and hard work to be effective. It structured the mind and helped to develop better reasoning skills.

Further, Dad would elaborate on the fact that the

reader's experience of interpreting a letter transported them into the writer's world and the experience was enhanced if the writer wrote in cursive. Although, cursive writing may be hard for some individuals to read, it reflects the personality of the writer and provides a deeper meaning of what is being conveyed. The shape of the letters, the size of the words and the idiosyncrasies of how letters are written communicate a uniqueness of the writer's thoughts and ultimately provides meaning to the reader. This uniqueness in communication conveys more than just the words themselves. When the reader interprets cursive writing, it encourages thoughtful understanding of the sentences. Writing was second nature to my father and Aunt Sarah. He loved corresponding with her.

During that trip, he voiced a concern to me "Larry, keep your mind active. Don't retire too soon. I made that mistake." He recalled the story, when as Vice Principal at Roosevelt High School, he grew tired of being the disciplinarian. He had to call parents and discuss student's poor academic performance or behavioral problems.

FAILING MEMORY

Dad excelled at his job. As a result, there were students who jeered at him in the hallway, some feared him and often parents hated him. The teachers and administrators admired him, because he worked hard to squelch or contain difficult disciplinary cases. Teachers were free to do what they do best; teach. However the roll of being a disciplinarian took a toll on him and Dad made the decision to retire early.

One day, after he decided to retire, Frank Hanson, the Franklin High School Principal, called him. Dad recounted his conversation to me, "Frank told me, Travis I want you to come back to Franklin as Vice Principal." Flattered, Dad remained committed to his retirement pledge. He told him, "I'm sorry, Frank but I'm planning on retiring at the end of this year. I've made up my mind." He continued in confidence, "I need a break. The vice principal's position at Roosevelt, while a good position, is wearing on me. The disciplinarian role is tough. I'd like to take you up on your offer, but I think it is time for me to leave the Seattle School District." Dad parenthetically told me, "And that was that." Frank responded, "Well, I can't say I'm not disappointed, but I fully understand. You need to do what is best for you." A year later, Frank retired as well.

Dad pondered, "You know I think Frank tried to tell me something that day. I think, he wanted me to go back to Franklin so when he retired I would be in a good position to become Principal at Franklin. I wish I hadn't been so hasty." He continued, "I think I could have enjoyed being Principal keeping my brain active."

***

When Dad retired, he wanted to enter the real-estate business full time. He had a partner, an educator, Johnny Walker. I thought Dad joked when he told me his name, but Mr. Walker was a real person in Dad's life. Johnny and Dad invested in properties together on several occasions and had made some money on the side. When Dad retired, he believed that he would be able to devote more time to his properties, assure the rentals stayed in good order, collect rent and sell the properties when the time looked right. He felt he could remain active.

In reality, the real estate business did not take off

like Dad had hoped. He purchased properties as far north as Rockport and as far east as Roslyn and Ronald, Washington. Financially, my Dad was "stretched thin." He did not have the cash for more investments. Johnny went on to other things and the partnership dissolved. However, Dad maintained the properties he owned. He loaned money to his children and felt good that he was able to help us from time to time.

Most of what Dad touched turned into figurative gold. As an example, when he came to Pendleton in the spring of 1994, toward the end of his real estate ventures, he talked to me about investing. Although, I remained skeptical, he said, "Larry, I think Pendleton is ripe for development. I'd like to buy some property in this booming real estate market with you and gain a return on our investment." I decided to play along. I said, "A retired guy from our church became a real estate agent in town. I think he might be able to help us." So, with enthusiasm, we left the house to talk to our agent. He showed us not one vacant lot with a nice view but four near the top of the hill. We could buy any or all the lots. I suggested that we start out small. Dad got serious and said let's take two. We purchased both lots for $10,000 total ($5000 each). Dad knew a bargain when he saw one. He said, "Larry, I'll purchase both lots and when we sell it we can split any profits." That offer, pleased me; a deal too good to be true. I invested nothing. When Dad sat down with the agent and wrote out a check, just like that, I was amazed. We felt the deal fell into our laps.

The two vacant lots were filled with grass and sagebrush that overlooked the North Hill and Reith Hill to the west. Forestry was in my blood. For more than ten years, I worked at the Timber and Lands section of a railroad company and at a local government as a Forest and Range Manager. I felt the lots needed to have at least a bush or tree on them. I obtained a handful of small pine saplings to plant on the property and talked to the neighbor about paying him a monthly sum to use some water to sprinkle the trees daily. I envisioned my own forest on these city lots, in the middle of the desert, where the only thing that grew well was wheat. My forest became a mini-project. It was located near the freeway on the south side of town at the top of a hill. The lots had good access to electricity from a nearby power pole, water, sewer and natural gas in the street. It would make a good home site for someone. I think, Dad hoped that I had intentions to build on the property. That was not in my plans. Still, I viewed it as an investment without risk. I expected someone to drive by, see the trees and think that it would be a nice place for a house.

After babying the trees for about a month, our real estate agent called me out of the blue and said, "Larry, you know those lots you just purchased? Are you interested in selling them? I have another buyer." I asked, "What is he offering?" The agent said, "Name your price." I smiled. "Let me talk to my father." I called Dad and told him about the potential sale. Dad said, "By all means. Do you think we could double our money?"

I said, "I don't know, but the agent said we could name our price." Dad replied, "Then, let's sell the lots together and offer both the lots for $22,000. That includes an additional 10% for the realtor and title fees and see what they say?" I said, "Okay then." I asked, "What if they only want one of the lots? Do we sell just one?" Dad said, "No, let's sell them both. The lots are small and they will want both lots to build something substantial anyway. We can always reconsider if they turn us down." I responded, "I'll call the agent."

I called and we received the full price we wanted for the lots. I was elated that I had received the quickest $5,000 that I ever earned without investing any money. Dad grinned too, pocketing his extra $5,000, as well as making back the money he originally invested and then some.

***

In 1997, Dad made an appointment to visit his doctor with a list of complaints. He was concerned about his impotence, high blood pressure and a host of other issues. In short, all at once, it seemed like his body was falling apart. Also, he was diagnosed with early signs of dementia.

His real estate and stock market investments had been good to him, but in 1997, he began the arduous task of consolidating his land and stock holdings.

My father knew about real estate, but the more property he owned the more his income taxes became complicated. Earlier, he hired a tax accountant to help him "square away" his books. Dad's complicated real estate and stock portfolio became difficult to manage in terms of the tax laws. He owed the IRS some money and decided to use the tax accountant on a regular basis. By 1997, he still had a good portfolio but it was pretty scattered. He began to realize his limitations. As an example, he ended up selling the Roslyn and Ronald, WA properties and began moving assets into mutual funds.

I think my dad reflected on his financial situation since he retired and was disappointed. His steady income were the pension and social security checks that he received. This income was not high enough for him to invest his money as he had done in the past. His memory began slipping and he could not readily keep track of what was needed to take place with the investments.

***

Dad always liked doing crossword puzzles. Now, because he had been diagnosed with dementia, it was important to him to show patience and perseverance when performing a task. He took up the puzzles in earnest, to keep his mind active. He liked vocabulary words and enjoyed figuring them out. Also, he, like my siblings and I, enjoyed doing jigsaw puzzles with the pieces spread out on a coffee or card table. As a family when I was a youth, we worked for hours trying to fit the puzzle piece together to create the final full picture. It provided us with a sense of a special talent, when we were able to find the small piece of the larger puzzle. My father developed a renewed interest in all these puzzles that we had and it seemed to be more important than ever to him.

***

In the spring of 1999, I returned to the Seattle area from Oregon. My father said, "Larry, why don't you take a walk with me."

I said, "Great. I'd love to."

I had no idea what he had in mind for me. We put on our hats and coats and started out the front door. Just outside of the house, rhododendrons bloomed with brilliant dark red lush flowers juxtaposed on a background of large waxy green leaves that were from the plant. I noticed the fragrance as we stepped onto the porch. The sweet smell permeated the air, but I found it difficult to tell if the rhododendron or the daffodils in the garden next to the house produced the scent. The bright yellow daffodils gave a stark contrast to the rhody's. We continued to walk down the street. Everything appeared to be in bloom. The birds sang and the old crow high in the Douglas fir cawed as we walked by the tree. He must have thought we invaded his territory. Dad theorized that the bird was hungry and hoped we would toss him a bread crumb or something when we returned.

We chit chatted and talked about springtime in Seattle. It was truly a joyous time of the year with a lot of promise ahead. We talked about the new growth and the plants that seemed to get greener with every day. But, something nagged Dad, I could tell; something significant bothered him and he wanted to get it out. I had this odd feeling, considering the discussion we just had about spring and new life. He tried to find the right words to make a transition from one topic to another but could not at that moment.

We walked down to Bothell Way, crossed at the

light as the cars stopped for the cross traffic. Dad and I found the Burke-Gilman Trail which was located across the highway along Lake Washington. We started walking along the Burke-Gilman Trail, which was paved. People were riding bikes, walking, running and exercising along its straight, narrow route. Log Boom Park became our destination which was about a mile from Lake Forest Park where we entered the trail. The heavy traffic noise from Bothell Way subsided. Again, we could hear the birds, happy sounds of joggers and bikes as they passed us. The sunlight glistened over Lake Washington as we observed watercraft that moved back and forth over the water. The only negative words out of Dad's mouth came as joggers or riders on bikes passed us on the path. They would yell out, "On your left," or ring their bells on the bikes to warn us they wanted to pass. He mocked them, by saying in a higher than normal voice, "On your left, on your left." He was somewhat annoyed that they were passing him, but then he would return to his nature of being positive.

Abruptly, he turned the conversation to his current life. He said, "I don't know why, but I stopped tutoring at the local high school. The principal encouraged me to continue, but I told her I couldn't. I guess I was lazy." I found this statement difficult to understand; I knew he wasn't lazy. Dad loved reaching into young minds and drawing out their personality and thinking abilities. He continued to be good at his method of teaching students. I queried him more about why he quit.

Dad said, "I just can't keep up the pace. I find myself not adding value to the student and his studies." I was perplexed because this did not sound like my father. Later, I realized that he tried to explain his thinking abilities had waned. He was not able to draw out the answer for the child. Maybe, he did not know the answer himself and therefore did not know how to guide the student. Whichever the reason, sadly I knew how much he loved teaching. I wondered aloud, if he just kept at it, would his own cognitive abilities improve or at the "very least" be maintained to last longer? Maybe he quit too early?

Finally, Dad said, "There is something I've wanted to tell you for some time now. I just haven't found the way or courage. I visited the doctor a while back and now it is confirmed that I have a form of Alzheimer's or dementia, the same disease your grandmother had."

I was stunned. I remember visiting my grandmother when she stayed at the nursing home in Bothell. She asked me the repetitive questions and I gave her the same answers each time. I recalled her concern about handling all those boys at Moses Brown when they returned to school. I saw the fear in her eyes as she pictured herself waiting for them and the realization that she was unable to do the things she had in the past.

When Dad told me he had also developed vascular dementia like Grandmother, I was devastated. I did not want him to suffer like Grandmother. I did not want him to restrict his activities, where he could go, what he could do and how he needed to act. He always appeared to be a superhero, or at least my superhero. Superheroes solve problems, remain the person with the answers that you need, or is the man you seek for some sort of advice. He gave me perspectives in my life that not only changed his life but began to change mine as well. *Grief set in.*

Dazed, the beautiful and bright walk with him

seemed to take a dark turn. The future lost its rose color and light vanished during this bright sunny day. I did not know what to say. I could only listen with few or no questions. It was like a bomb dropping a few steps in front of me. I felt a deep responsibility to hold on to him, keep him safe, and not only him but my family too.

Dad tried to be reassuring. He said, "I'm not worried. It is just something I will be going through and I want you to know. I am not remembering things like I once did."

Still in denial, I protested, "But, we all do not remember things and you seem to be doing well now."

He said, "No it is confirmed by the doctor, I have dementia." He reiterated, to further reassure me, he said, "I'm not worried. I'll just take it as it comes. It'll just happen."

I responded hopefully, "Medicines can cure it, right? Science has come so far." My denial scared me as much as the disease.

He said, "No, there is no cure. The tangles and plaques develop in the brain and science doesn't know why they form nor how to resolve it. When severe, the brain atrophies and the neurons and synapses don't function like they once did. They don't know you have Alzheimer's disease for sure until they do an autopsy. Some medicines seem to help you cope with the disease but they only help with some memory retention and do not prevent or delay the disease."

Afterward, I endured silence for several steps as we continued walking all the way down to Log Boom Park and I could once again hear the buses and auto traffic along the roadway above the trail. We turned around and headed back toward the direction from which we came down. It was the Burke-Gilman trail.

He reiterated, "It'll be okay. I'm prepared for what happens." But, I still wasn't sure.

CHAPTER 12 - LIVING WITH DEMENTIA

It was official. I had to recognize the fact and come to terms with the idea of my Dad having dementia. I could no longer dismiss his words when he said "Larry, I am forgetting things." Yet, he was at ease with the disease.

During the summer of 1999, I did not understand his situation. I hoped Dad would remain independent. To me, he appeared to be the same person. I did not see any outward signs of dementia. He seemed to be sharp with a good sense of humor and was able to articulate his needs, wants and desires. From my father's viewpoint, his conversations flowed, he kept his disease and his current predicament in perspective. The continuity in his life covered up any signs of his illness.

When I made comments to him about his wellbeing, I kept a positive attitude and complemented him on his abilities and the things he did on a daily basis. I might have said, "Dad, I'm amazed at how well you do those crossword puzzles," or "Dad, your letters to Aunt

Sarah are insightful and interesting," or "Dad, I want to know about your family of origin." Also, I noticed my father tried hard to be optimistic and joyful because it was generally second nature to him. However, from a realistic point of view I saw him have some memory lapses followed with elements of depression.

That summer and fall, I came to the conclusion that I had a limited amount of time to be with him. So, I decided to record the stories he told. I went to Lake Forest Park often to visit and learn from him. He could spin a yarn with the best of them. I wanted to know what he knew about our relatives. He told me stories about my grandfather, my dad's fondness of him, his art work, and working as a stockbroker through The Depression. This was despite the fact that he had an Art Degree from the prestigious Chicago Art Institute and his degree in engineering from Yale.

Grandfather lost all his money during The Depression. Additionally, Dad told me stories about the time my great grandmother required my grandmother to divorce my grandfather in the middle of that same Depression. Later they reunited in California and remarried after World War II. It seemed like the story books are made of and people really enjoy reading. I thought of it as the consummate love story.

Still, I wanted to know more about my father. I lived with this man for the first 18 years of my life, and I loved him dearly, but I still missed significant pieces of his life. As an example, he enlisted in the Army and joined the Army Air Corps during World War II. He never talked much about the war to me, my two brothers or sister when we were children. I suspect he did not want to glorify the war. However, Dad told war stories to the students at Denny Junior High School to keep their attention during class. He joked with friends about keeping the kids on the edge of their seats, but never really described any details to his own children. I did not know how he survived the many harrowing episodes he had during the war. Now, I wanted him to tell me some of those war stories. I did not know where to begin, so I began with his childhood and his father. Then, I expanded to his extended family. I compiled what I could before he could not articulate the stories anymore, but many unanswered questions remained.

At this time, Dad was still communicating ably, or at least he aptly covered up his inability to problem solve. Mostly he seemed alert, but some days it became difficult for him.

One day, Dad attended a meeting in downtown Seattle. I do not recall why, but it could have been a meeting about his retirement with the Seattle School District, a meeting with a lawyer over some real estate deal or to the county courthouse as well as the county office building. Here's what I pieced together based on my knowledge of the trip that he took by himself.

***

Normally, it would have been a routine trip for him, albeit a little out of the ordinary. Dad drove his small Mazda truck without incident downtown Seattle, parked it under the freeway overpass, and found his meeting without issue. He attended the meeting, took sufficient notes and started to gather his things to return home. He could think clearly in the morning and he could figure out where he needed to be and maneuver efficiently through the city maze. But, in the afternoon, he had many things on his mind and must have found it difficult to think clearly.

He reached into his pocket, found his truck keys and set off to retrieve his vehicle and head home. There was just one problem. He could not remember where he parked his little white pickup truck. After walking all over downtown Seattle, Dad remembered he parked under a bridge but he could not draw from his mind an image of where he parked, nor could he remember the bridge and direction from the meeting room he needed to go. He wandered the city for about two hours trying to envision what the area looked like and where he parked the vehicle but to no avail. Dad headed southeast down 6th Avenue looking in the parking lots under the freeway with the viaduct above. He walked to Yesler Avenue until he realized that he had gone too far. Then, he turned around and walked back through each parking lot but still could not find his truck. The more he looked the fewer things looked familiar. Finally, after looking high and low for his vehicle he gave up.

It turned dusk, became late and Dad started having trouble seeing as well as remembering. At that point, he decided he needed to find another form of transportation because dinner time was approaching. He felt that it was prudent to consider alternatives; since it was now rush hour. Dad remembered he had rode the bus and had money in his pocket. However, he just wasn't clear where and what bus to take.

Dad remembered previously, he caught express buses that took him to Lake Forest Park and when he reached the appropriate location, he could just walk up the hill from the bus stop. It seemed to be an easy fix for the night and he planned to come back in the morning and find his pickup.

Dad headed down the sidewalk to Marion Street and 2nd Avenue. He went across the street to the bus stop, purchased a ticket and hopped on a bus that said express. On that crowded bus, a nice young man stood up and gave Dad his seat. He accepted gratefully and finally relaxed. Sitting helped Dad regain strength because he had walked so far. His feet hurt and the walk had tired him out. Dad eyed the young man as he got off the bus about two stops later. The young man waved to Dad as he departed and Dad waved back settling into his seat. He hoped to be home soon.

The bus traveled through an area that was unfamiliar to Dad. On this day, what was "unfamiliar" had become the norm for him. He was not worried. Once he got closer to home, he knew he would recognize the streets and "do what he had to do." He replayed the events of the day in his mind and still wondered where he parked his vehicle. It did not matter, because for now, he was safe on the bus. As it got darker, he was glad that someone else was driving. He knew he did not drive well at night. His cataracts obscured his vision and that made everything appear to be cloudy. The bus took some twists and turns and finally got onto the freeway. Thinking that it would not be long now before, "I am home." Dad closed his eyes and tried to doze, but the noise and rumble of the glass windows on the bus kept him awake. Every once in a while, he would open his eyes and see buildings or pavement flash by. When he closed his eyes and opened them again, Dad thought that he saw an airport. He chose to ignore this sighting.

Dad may have dozed again, but this time with his eyes open, he heard the driver boom out the out the words, "Federal Way, next stop." Now, that was a shock. "Federal Way," he must have heard that wrong. Federal Way was far to the south, which was in the opposite direction he wanted to go. It could not be right. The driver made some turns and ended the ride at a bus stop. Passengers piled off. The station did not look familiar. Dad stayed on the bus. He was not sure of much of anything these days and especially the last few hours. Through the haze in his mind, he had the first real inkling that he might be in trouble. At the next stop, about half the bus emptied and very few passengers got on.

The bus driver closed the door and began to take off. A couple of turns and they were back on the freeway. Dad tried to "settle in." Again, the bus left the freeway, found a major road, and sped down it which led to another freeway. The bus crossed this road and passed the "Outlet Collection; Seattle."

The bus driver's voice boomed this time with the words, "Next Stop Auburn." Now, Dad was aware of the fact that he made a serious mistake and needed to get off the bus. This must be the southern express and he wanted to go north. He needed to find another bus that was going in the right direction. Dad was perplexed but determined that he would find his way home.

Dad knew Mother would be worried. It was likely that she had determined he met someone and wanted to go to coffee with them. Often, he befriended people and was delayed because he liked to talk, but it was uncharacteristic of him to forget the time as well as his responsibilities at home. It nagged at him. He knew Mother expected him to arrive home around 6:00 p.m. because his meeting should have ended at 3.

Dad talked to the driver and he told him the number of the next bus he needed to take that was headed north to Lake Forest Park. It was getting late. The bus driver said the last bus leaving Auburn is at 6:30 p.m. It goes to Renton, but from there it goes up the east side of Lake Washington to Bellevue and Redmond, and not to Lake Forest Park. From Renton, he needed to double-back downtown. Dad climbed aboard the last bus from Auburn to Renton per the instructions he had received from the driver. Dad realized that the directions he had been given and understood were already becoming "muddled" in his head. Since, he was less familiar with the southern part of Seattle and it was late as well as dark, he became a little anxious.

Dad struggled to solve his problem, tried to keep his wits and not panic. He knew he had to ask questions and rely on others. In the past, he was not afraid to ask questions. Dad sensed that he had to rely upon others for help because darkness had set in, he was traveling an unfamiliar route and this was necessary for him to survive. The bright lights on the buildings of the businesses they traveled passed made him squint and the neon signs "stabbed" him in the eyes at times. Trees adorned the side of the street and it was surprising how black it could be traveling though noncommercial areas. He was not sure where he was, but had been told he was headed to Renton.

From that point, he would be able to negotiate the King County Metro Bus System, but would need help from bystanders and bus drivers. He planned to ask questions until he got the answers he needed; "trusting people along the way." He listened for the bus driver to say "Next stop Renton" and immediately Dad got off the bus when it arrived at Bay One Renton Transit Center. It was nearly 7:30 in the evening. Where did he go from here?

Dad thought hard, asked experienced bus drivers questions and concluded, "I want to go back to Seattle to catch the Lake Forest Park express bus." Again, he reminded himself that was the way he knew and others had advised him to go that way as well. It was getting late and he had no idea when the buses ran and what time they stopped at night. He asked a bus driver on a smoke break what bus he should catch to downtown Seattle. The bus driver said, "Catch the Metro 101. At Jackson and 4th catch the 522." Dad wrote the numbers down on a piece of scrap paper, and thanked him. He looked for Metro 101. Through asking some additional questions, he learned he had about 20 minutes to kill and found he needed to walk to and wait at Bay 5 which was not too far away. He found a nice middle aged lady to talk to while he waited. Also, she had planned on taking a trip into Seattle. When the bus arrived they all boarded and he set off to Seattle again; back to where he had started his "bus adventure."

About 8:13 p.m., he boarded the 101. It was an

older bus, not an express like the one he had taken earlier. Dad thought, "This would do." "Just get me to downtown Seattle where I catch the correct bus that goes back to Lake Forest Park." Dad lost his self-confidence. He had relied on strangers and the directions they gave him in the hope that he would be home soon. Therefore, he concentrated on the important questions he needed to ask to help his disoriented mind. The night continued to be very dark outside the bus, but now the city lights began to comfort him. The bus seemed to stop many more times along this route than the other bus ride. Exhausted, he discovered a lack of friendly faces on the bus. Most of the people read their newspapers or books, slept or just looked outside as the city life passed by them. Really, no one spoke. Dad exchanged polite short conversations with several riders before everything returned to being silent, except for the rattle of windows and the surging transmission of the bus when it stopped or accelerated. Dad tried to close his eyes, but remained fitful and a little scared. As the bus wound downtown, it looped to the underground tunnel. He would hear names like "Next stop, International District/China Town." He was tired and did not know where to get off to catch his next bus, when he heard "Fourth and Jackson at King Street Station." The bus driver looked at Dad and said, "This is your stop. Time to get off." He took his cue and Dad prepared to leave the Metro 101. He stepped off the bus onto the platform. Knowing that he needed to change buses, Dad found his scrap of paper that said "522." Bus 522 must be the Lake Forest Park express bus. He looked at signs and asked questions about the 522 bus to people who were "passersby."

Dad found a nice man who spoke broken English, but he was not sure of the instructions he had been given, so he asked a lady. She pointed to the board that showed the 522 schedule and said, "That is the bus you want." He waited until he saw the 522 bus and it said, "Woodinville" on its reader-board. Woodinville is three towns further along the route passed Lake Forest Park. He knew she had given him proper instructions. The lady came up to Dad and said, "This is it," so he boarded the bus. The bus continued down 4th street. This bus driver boomed out, "Next stop, King County District Court, 4th and James," "Next Stop Columbia Center, Fourth and

Cherry," and finally "Westlake Park, 4th and Pike." The bus turned up Pike Street and lumbered to 8th Avenue then turned on Olive Way. As he sat on the bus, Dad recognized some of the names of the streets but still could not be certain of the pathway the bus was traveling. He started to ask questions of other passengers. Often, he would receive a strange look or a curt answer. He could not afford another mistake. It was approaching 9 p.m.

Finally, feeling a little dejected, Dad's confusion was apparent. The young lady who was sitting next to him said, "We'll be on the freeway soon. I promise. You'll be okay, and I'll let you know when we get close to Lake Forest Park." Dad was grateful for the help, and he realized that things were finally looking up. The lady had offered him some help and lent a friendly face.

The bus climbed toward the freeway. Finally, Dad saw some familiar landscape as they approached and entered the freeway that was headed north this time. He gained some self-assurance as the bus crossed over the waterway that connects Lake Washington to Union Bay. He saw the familiar University of Washington commercial area near the freeway. Then, the bus left the freeway passing by the somewhat familiar Green Lake commercial district. He thought he remembered several stops along Lake City Way, which eventually became Bothell Way at 145th Street that he knew fairly well. At least now, he saw surroundings more clearly and knew he was on the correct bus. It was not long before the bus made to Shoreline near his home. He knew he needed to get off at the next stop. Dad was elated that he remembered this familiar territory. His adrenaline surged as he thought he might find his way home in spite of being tired. As he approached, it was just a matter of time before the bus would be stopping and he would be getting off. He did not need to have the bus driver tell him. The pleasant young lady sitting next to him nudged his elbow and said, "This is your stop," as the driver said forcefully, "Next stop 170th and Bothell Way." Dad gathered what few belongings he had, looked out the window to see the local coffee shop near his home, and thanked the lady and driver profusely as he exited the bus. He could hardly wait to see his spouse.

When Dad arrived at the bus stop, it was 9:34 p.m. He knew to cross Bothell Way and hike up the hill to the house. His tiredness gave way to exhilaration. He was exhausted from his day's adventures and his blood now surged through his body at an exciting speed. It took forever for the light to change and when it did, he bounded across the highway like a 20 year old kid. Dad arrived at the first hill and finally felt his age as he continued to climb. Even with the adrenaline shooting through his bloodstream, he had to stop half way up. He began to trudge home; one foot in front of the other.

Dad crossed the street at the top of the hill. Then, he headed and then up 174th Street for the last long block near the house.

It was 9:45 p.m. when he arrived home, could not find his key and had to knock on the door.

Meanwhile, Mother had not sat idly by. She contacted my brothers. First, she called my brother, Mike, to see if by chance Dad had stopped at his house or called him for some reason. Mike had not heard from him. Then, she called Steve, and he had not heard either. Mother thought she might have to call the police.

When she heard the knock, Mother came running

to the door, opened it and gave my father a big hug. "I was so worried about you. Where have you been? I called Mike and Steve and some of the neighbors. I nearly called the police. Mike started to get ready to look for you." Dad couldn't get a word in edgewise, when Mother asked "Have you had anything to eat? Are you hungry?" Dad finally responded, "A little."

Dad was famished, but mostly exhausted and happy to be home. Through the misadventures and the excitement of being home he forgot he was hungry until he was reminded by Mother. She gave him a sandwich and she called Mike to let him know Dad was home. Meanwhile, Steve stopped by the house to support Mother, greeted Dad and gave him a big hug too.

Dad was amazed with himself. He solved his problem; he found his way home.

That night, Dad slept well and the next day all he wanted to do was rest, look out his picture window and enjoy life. Finding his vehicle did not enter his mind, nor did he think anything unusual had happened to him the night before. Grateful to be home, he did not want more misadventures and he simply put things out of his mind. Mother and Steve queried Dad later that morning as to what he remembered. Obviously, Dad had a general notion about what had happened and even a foggier notion about where he may have parked his small pickup truck. As Dad tried hard to recount his story, he thought it must be parked under a bridge downtown. Mother listened intensely. Dad's adventure home became somewhat of a mystery to him and he was puzzled why he was being asked so many questions. He just knew he was home. Mother called her friend Jean, and they went downtown to locate Dad's pickup truck in order to bring it back to Lake Forest Park.

After, searching the downtown area for some time, they did not find the vehicle parked anywhere Dad had vaguely described. Finally, they ended up contacting an impound lot, found his truck and paid the bill. Jean drove the pickup back to Lake Forest Park and Mother followed her. Once again, life became whole and everyone relaxed.

CHAPTER 13 - 50TH WEDDING ANNIVERSARY

I learned about Dad's "lost truck experience," the weekend I arrived in Seattle which followed the incident. Everyone involved expressed their shock because our father had always been alert with a command of his surroundings and had few mishaps of this nature. The dementia must have contributed to his disorientation. I think from Dad's perspective, it scared him. For the rest of us, we did not care to see this situation repeated. Therefore, whether it was right or wrong, we all became more protective of our father.

In the fall of 1999, we realized that Dad needed to feel he was independent and a functioning member of society, despite his dementia; especially in the early stages. Establishing that independence was a hard balance because it was like raising children. You do not want them to inadvertently harm themselves. We needed to learn how to weigh Dad's ability to make mistakes but at the same time keep him safe. It took more than just Mother to do this for our father.

Larry Calkins

Dad needed to use his mind or it would atrophy. He continued to be diligent about his mental health which included problem solving abilities. He walked and exercised on a regular basis, which kept his body fit. Also, he continued to solve crossword puzzles, read and write. Willingly, he did projects for Mother around the house. Dad wanted to continue to be optimistic and have an "upbeat life" for as long as it was possible.

***

One day, during another visit, I went to the bank with Dad. I suggested that he may want to withdraw money because the family had planned to attend an event. I thought, he should have a "few" dollars with him if he decided to buy something to eat. I wanted to give him as much latitude as I could by allowing him to make decisions which I felt would generate good mental health.

Dad agreed with me that he may need some money and decided to make a withdrawal from his account at the bank.

The employees at the bank greeted my father by his name. Everyone in the Lake Forest Park branch participated in this delightful small town custom. Since, they knew my father and mother well, I introduced myself but stayed in the background. Dad went to the counter and pulled his debit card out of his wallet and said, "Larry how much do you think I need to withdraw?" That became an opportunity that I squandered because of what happened next. "I can't help you with that Dad. You need to decide," was my reply. At the time, I was mistaken and thought I had no business telling or even suggesting what he may need. Dad said, "Okay then, $500." He gave the teller his card and withdrew $500. I did not say a word in order to protect him from being embarrassed.

When we returned home, I needed to tell my mother what happened and she knew what to do in order to correct Dad's decision. A little later Mother and Dad were alone downstairs and she asked him, "Did you withdraw some money out of the bank?" Dad said, "Yes." She asked, "How much?" He opened his wallet and showed her the $500. She suggested, "I think that's too much money but you can keep $20 for today and I'll deposit the balance back into the bank." He objected, saying, "I don't want to be humiliated when you take the money back to the bank and redeposit it in front of the bank personnel." Immediately, she understood his fear and said, "I'll take it to the Kenmore Branch not far away and no one will be the wiser." I was glad Dad relented and Mother solved my problem in an easy and succinct conversation. She saved face for father and son.

All three of us were relieved. Dad had his $20 and his dignity. I kept my self-respect and Mother worked a miracle. Now, it is true that everyday living had its challenges. As my wife says, "We do the best with the tools and knowledge we have, at the time." I have a hard time remembering that fact.

***

On Wednesday mornings, Mother and Dad joined friends from the old neighborhood for breakfast at a local Café off of Bothell Way. The friends would reminisce about the old times, when my parent's young family lived on 195th Street in Kenmore. Also, they talked about the day's events and current affairs.

One Wednesday, I went with them, and

reconnected with old neighbors. Dad relished getting out, interacting with people who knew him and he felt comfortable being himself around them. Most importantly, it gave him the opportunity to engage in light conversation. If he wanted to be silent or talk, it was okay. At the end of the meal, Bob and Harry our former neighbors and Dad rose from the table and wandered over to the counter to pay for the meal. Bob and Dad both had *dementia*. Quick witted Harry watched carefully as the two paid their portion. As they prepared to pay the bills, both Bob and Dad opened their wallets tenuously and took out twenty dollars; each to pay for the meals. Harry assured both Bob and Dad that they had received the proper change. He did this without causing a scene. Mother and Bob's wife let the men handle the cash.

Later, I asked Mother about what had transpired. She said, "It gives Dad a sense of responsibility and control over his day to day activities, which is something he rarely has now. I *salt* his wallet with cash so that he will have the proper amount to cover the payment for meals." Silently, she helped Dad without him knowing.

***

That fall, my brothers, sister and I cooked up the idea of having a 50th wedding anniversary celebration for Dad and Mom. It would honor them, the years they lived together and acknowledge their love for one another.

A quarter century earlier, we held their 25th anniversary celebration at my Aunt Eva's house. My mother was the second oldest of six children. There were three boys and three girls in the family. Aunt Eva was the youngest girl. At that time, she graciously hosted the event and planned to keep it as a surprise party by inviting Dad and Mother to come to her house for dinner one Sunday evening.

I remember, Aunt Eva happily arranged the intimate, joyous affair. She organized nearly everything. My sister and I sent out a few invitations to some of our parent's closest friends. Other than that, we did not have to "lift a finger" to help her. Aunt Eva asked us to be quiet about the surprise party.

As far as Mother and Dad knew, the event would be a small simple Sunday dinner. If they suspected something, we did not know it because of the expressions on their faces. The place looked festive and the guests greeted them with gracious accolades. The happy couple expressed pleasure reconnecting with friends and family. I brought my fledgling family from Oregon and met my sister, Alva, who came with Mom and Dad. Steve and Mike were both in the Army and they could not get away. Of course, my younger cousins, Aunt Eva's children were also there. Aunt Eva carried the day!

Unlike the 25th anniversary celebration, the 50th celebration could not be a surprise because we invited many more people. All my siblings, Steve, Mike, Alva and I attended with our growing families. We invited old neighbors, new neighbors, friends of our parents and of course we also invited our aunts, uncles and cousins, as well as their families. We did not expect most of the relatives to come because they did not live around the Seattle area and it would have been a long trip for them. However, Aunt Eva said, "your cousins and I will definitely come to the event, and we wouldn't have missed it for the world."

We needed a venue that would work for this celebration, and Alva had a friend who suggested a popular restaurant in the area. We chose a Saturday afternoon in January, 2000 with a no host dinner. We prepared and sent out the invitations.

My nerves got the better of me, but Dad's nerves must have been raw. I had never seen my father become self-conscious about himself as I did prior to this event. Most of the time, his self-assurance prevailed, but today was different. He fussed with his tie and coat because he wanted to leave a good impression. He was not sure about his memory, abilities or appearance. Also, I imagined that he was nervous about meeting longtime friends and whether they would notice he displayed signs of someone who suffered with dementia. I remember him asking Mother if he looked okay. Mother reassured him by saying, "Yes Travis. You look great." My mother had always been nurturing, but this time she knew why my father was self-conscious. His new behavior caused us to take notice and we all wanted to help him cope in this situation. Mother never dwelt on his concerns, but was not dismissive either. Intuitively, she began taking on more of a lead role in their relationship, guarding against being overly protective, allowing him to make mistakes and still providing support. I learned from my mother, trying to follow her lead; all the while being impressed by her abilities.

We arrived at the restaurant in separate vehicles. Dad and Mother drove their own car. My wife, Carrie, daughter, Emma, and I in another. Marcella, our middle daughter, came separately from Oregon State University. Hettie, our oldest daughter and her family came from Pullman. Carrie, Emma and I stayed at Carrie's father's house. Marcella, Hettie and Brian (Hettie's husband) stayed with my parents.

When everyone arrived, we ordered dinner, ate and enjoyed each other's company. It was a booth type setting. Although, the restaurant catered our party in a roped off section, we pretty much ate as separate family units. Emma, my daughter, took pictures to document the event. After everyone finished eating dinner, we opened up the celebration.

There were a large number of people who gathered around Mother and Dad, but some stayed in the booths where they could see what was occurring. Mother and

Dad opened their 50th wedding anniversary gifts.

Mother and Dad took a bite of the anniversary cake on their forks and with arms intertwined gently placed the cake in the mouth of one

another. This was a true wedding anniversary celebration. It was a joyous moment. The guests did a lot of laughing, clapping and guffawing over their experience. Family members renewed old acquaintances and new friendships were created. Generally speaking, I think the event served its purpose because it was wonderful to bring friends and family together for a pleasant time and a fun event.

Most importantly, Mother seemed pleased and made favorable comments about the evening. Dad wanted to show his gratitude too. His nervousness was put to rest. He thanked the guests for coming and his children for sponsoring the event. His gracious and thoughtful nature returned. There were no quips or jokes in his well delivered speech; just gratefulness.

Larry Calkins

CHAPTER 14 - MEXICAN RIVIERA

In May 2000, Carrie and I lived in Bend, Oregon. Emma, our youngest daughter, attended college in Tacoma. Our older two children either worked or began graduate studies. I worked for the State of Oregon as an Air Quality Specialist, and one Friday morning I organized a work-related meeting with people from the City of The Dalles and key organizations. This included community leaders, representatives from the fire and health departments as well as those involved with industrial sources of air pollution. We explored methods of improving air quality including ideas to limit burning in woodstoves and burn barrels on poor air quality days.

I felt good about the discussion but could not wait to get home. I anticipated a visit from Mother and Dad and expected a 3 hour drive back to Bend. I intended to return to my office, drop off my work vehicle and then leave early to return home and wait for my parents. When the meeting finished, I left about 1:00 p.m. and started driving down Highway 97 on the east side of the Cascade Mountains.

Earlier that week, I talked to Mother and Dad. I encouraged them to come to Bend for a visit. They agreed and decided to make the trip an adventure. Mother made reservations at a hotel in Redmond, Oregon which is about a 20 minute drive to Bend. She sent me her itinerary.

As I zipped out of The Dalles, the road became a blur. I drove on autopilot and started thinking about Mother and Dad's visit as well as planning upcoming events. I was worried that they would arrive at the house before me.

The road from The Dalles wound up and down hills. The Dalles is situated right on the Columbia River at 109 feet in elevation at the river and rises to about 600 feet in elevation at the southern edges of town. I began the trip back to Bend by driving through a few cherry orchards until the scenery gave way to grass and sage surroundings. Cattle roamed the grass and sage lands and it is not uncommon to see mule deer along the route.

FAILING MEMORY

The tree line of the Cascade Mountains to the west became evident looking off in the distance where a dark green patch of trees snaked around the mountains. The rugged skyline appeared as I looked to the horizon. I climbed to an elevation of 1600 feet and then the road dropped down a winding highway. This led toward the outdoor recreation town of Maupin and into the Deschutes River Valley. Maupin offers entry locations for rubber rafting or boating down the Deschutes River. Crossing a bridge to the other side of the Deschutes River, I drove up switchbacks scaling another steep hill to the plateau on top at roughly an elevation of 3000 feet. The road straightened out and I was able to see down the plateau for some distance.

As I continued driving down the straight unbending roadway, it was strange to see a small white Mazda pickup off to the side of the road; far up the roadway. I was curious and planned to stop to see if there was a problem because few vehicles travel this stretch of the road. The cars that do are driven fairly fast. I slowed down to see what problem may have occurred. It was a wonderful surprise to see my mother and dad inside the

Mazda. I pulled over to greet them and they responded in a happy manner, but they were also surprised to see me along this desolate stretch of roadway. They did not have any problem with their truck. They happened to be looking at a map as I approached them with the inside car light on which they turned off as I spoke. I reassured them that they were on the right road and listed the next towns they would approach—Madras, then Redmond and finally Bend. I expressed an urgency to return to the office so I could finalize my work day early and go home to greet them when they arrived.

I raced to the office and then home. An hour later Mother and Dad showed up at the house after checking into their hotel. We ate a nice dinner and talked until they went back to the hotel that evening.

Unbeknownst to me, that afternoon the Oregon Department of Transportation rerouted traffic. Dad and Mother got lost and never found their hotel. They followed the road but did not know they needed to make an additional turn. Instead of traveling toward Redmond, they drove all the way to Sisters, Oregon.

FAILING MEMORY

Late the next morning they arrived at our house. After I received them at the door, Mother and Dad told us their saga. I was mortified. Also, Dad showed me hotel registration paperwork. Dad's name was on the paper and in the place where form said "company," he had written "spouse." We laughed at the thought of the hotel manager wondering what his company produced.

Somewhere in our conversation, Dad suggested that he would like to go on a trip someplace to see the world. Mother's silence could have cut "the air with a knife." I did not recognize the situation and I pressed on with my ideas. I suggested to my parents that they sit down and talk. I volunteered to be a mediator and made suggestions about where they could go, the mode of transportation to use and I offered to go on the trip with them.

Mother did not want to go on just any trip. She needed to consider her age, medical issues and mode of transportation that would not be too stressful. The most important issue that Mother had to face was Dad's dementia. He had to be in a place where he could navigate easily without great effort. She thought hard,

189

given her misgivings about any trip. Mother knew she would be making all the decisions for both of them. Dad would just be along for the ride.

After a while, Mother suggested that we go on a cruise. She wanted to have a bathroom of her own and be on an organized trip where the activities would be planned for us. This would limit the amount of problem solving for her and Dad. I understood her dilemma somewhat and happily accepted her solution.

I talked to Carrie and she agreed to go on the trip. We planned activities that we could do with my parents and on our own. Mother thought that would be fine. At least, I would be there to help entertain Dad throughout the trip. She suggested the Mexican Rivera and I agreed, wholeheartedly.

When Dad and Mother returned home, she contacted a tour group through a travel agent in Lake City which is a few miles from Lake Forest Park. The agent set up the cruise with other retired folks from Seattle and the group took the cruise with couples from similar backgrounds. Carrie, Mother, Dad and I planned to travel on a popular cruise line in November, 2000.

The four of us took a flight to San Diego, along with the other Lake City vacationers in order to catch the cruise ship. Little did I know at the time, that we would spend much of the vacation with the same group of people, sitting at the dining table for our meals.

I was amazed that so many people had arranged to go on the same trip. When we arrived in San Diego, there was a very long line that we had to stand-in before boarding the cruise ship and checking our bags.

I was glad as we moved along slowly in line and finally completed being processed. Then, we waited on the dock for them to call our room assignments prior to us entering the ship. Again, we waited elbow to elbow. When she organized the trip, Mother selected Carrie's and my room next to theirs. She booked us cheap interior rooms. These small rooms housed a full sized bed, a dresser and a small bathroom. The cramped quarters provided us with just enough room for two people to walk past one another.

When the toilets were flushed, the waste water

went down the hole in the bowl with such gusto that a comedian during his routine in a show imitated the sound of the flushing through the microphone. This caused the audience to roar with laughter.

Entertainment on the ship included comedians as head-liners, live bands with singers, a casino and swimming pool to just name a few activities. The cruise directors organized lectures with knowledgeable experts that explained about the cultures and places we were about to visit. Also, there were numerous restaurants and eating establishments. The small cabins demanded that we walk around the ship to avoid getting cabin fever. Further, this encouraged us to explore the ship.

We set off on our adventure. The first thing that the crew required of us was to "muster on deck." Everyone was called out of their cabins. We were placed in a line around the ship as the cruise director explained safety requirements and expectations on board. When excused, Dad, Mother, Carrie and I went to the main deck to look around. We walked through the casino on the way to the outer deck and stood near the railing and waved goodbye to San Diego as we anticipated the rest of the journey. The cool breeze blew through our hair and we fortunately brought light jackets along with us.

A day into the trip, the first port of call was Ensenada, Mexico. This started our full experience of being on a cruise ship and included an understanding of the Mexican community. Since it was Sunday, Carrie wanted to witness a Catholic Mass in Mexico and Mother decided she would like to go along with her. Dad and I decided to wander through the city and experience the flavor of Mexico. Most importantly, to walk and talk like we did often, in the past. As we walked, we discussed the trip, what we saw and other topics of the day. Dad seemed to take in the surroundings, but mostly was interested in my thoughts and what I had to say.

All of a sudden, I heard my name being called. Was it a mistake? I kept on walking and talking with Dad. Then, I heard my name being called again. I looked in an open air store and saw Tony. Tony worked with me in Bend, Oregon. What was he doing in Ensenada? The same thing as I was doing; only he drove there. We stopped talking and I introduced him to my father. I talked to him for a while to compare notes. We both could not believe we had traveled half-way down the Pacific Coast and met each other in another country. I had no idea he would be there. It was an odd but a memorable coincidence.

Our visit at Ensenada ended and we went back to the ship for more experiences. The next port-of-call occurred at Cabo San Lucas. At Cabo, we took a tour of the harbor. This time Carrie, Dad, Mother and I went together. We took a small boat through the iconic Arch of Cabo San Lucas (El Archo), saw Pelican Rock and Cannery Beach. It was a sunny happy day to remember. Both Dad and Mother appeared to have a good time because we talked among ourselves comparing notes about the experience thus far and our smiles and laughter expressed our relaxed state.

We boarded the cruise ship again and sailed to Puerto Vallarta. There, Dad and Mother planned to take a tour of the city, look at sculptures like the Malecon Puerto Vallarta and other interesting sites. They seemed to enjoy their experience together. Carrie and I signed up for a horse back experience that would eventually take us up a hill overlooking the port.

FAILING MEMORY

We left the ship and boarded a bus that took us through town which included a small residential neighborhood. There was a large barn on the outskirts of the city that housed the horses we would be riding. The tour guide instructed us on the procedures for stopping the horses if we should lose or drop something. I accepted the instructions we had been given, but it seemed to me that they were overly cautious. The instructor gave me a large horse to ride because of my height, which is 6 feet tall. He told me the horse was more spirited than some of the others. Carrie was given a gentle mare to ride that would easily as well as uneventfully get her up and down the hill. The animals paced themselves as they began walking up the slope. The mare and steed we had mounted along with the other riders on their horses settled into a methodical stride. It was a nice even pace, as the animals dutifully followed their counterparts that were in front of them.

To my surprise, pleasure and in a way disappointment, the horse that I was riding, started out on the trek as a pleasant well-behaved animal. All of the horses seemed to be obedient. I grew up with horses and felt that I could handle all but the most unruly ones. We arrived at the top of the hill, dismounted and the handlers took the reins of each horse. Carrie and I went to the scenic vista to see the city and ocean beyond. We spent ample time, about 30 minutes, at the top satisfying our curiosity and romantic notions about the view.

Then, the handlers asked us to mount back up for the return ride to the station where we would catch our bus back to the ship. As before, the horses let us mount them and we started to ride down the hill. It got slightly steeper as we descended and the horses began to trot which bounced us around. They stepped lively down the hill and once we were at the bottom they began to canter. This action caused us to bounce even further.

Then, it happened! My backpack zipper unzipped and my camera sprang out. I managed to stop my horse; not quite sure what had happened. One of the handlers came up from behind and handed the undamaged camera to me. He saw it land on the ground and rode his horse to catch up with me. I was very grateful, thanked him and allowed my horse to continue the ride. I looked for Carrie and she was far ahead with the other group of riders.

Well, my horse decided to make up for lost time. The other horses were cantering toward the barn. I was astonished when all of a sudden I was engaged in a wild ride. He was moving fast, actually galloping toward the barn which meant our arrival time was the same as the other horses. It was a jarring experience that is completely imbedded in my brain. It has been a story to tell my grandchildren. We boarded the bus and went back to the ship for the next leg of our adventure.

We met up with my parents, swapped stories and settled into our routine onboard the ship.

As the cruise commenced, Mother decided she wanted to go see an act that was performing near the swimming pool and asked for company. I made a mistake when I said to her that I wanted to do something else and did not express an interest in going to the show. Unfortunately, Dad agreed with me and Carrie decided to do something different as well. Mother's idea of having a companion going with her vanished. Neither Dad nor I would escort her.

Mother was visibly upset and stomped off from

Dad and I. She was left to fend for herself. I felt a strong desire to talk to Mother and smooth things out with her. I made sure Dad was comfortable and went to find Mother. I found her sitting on stairs that headed up to the deck where the swimming pool was located. When, I sat down beside Mother to talk, it became obvious to me from her demeanor, that she was depressed. I expressed my regret for making the decision not to accompany her to the show. If I did accompany her, I knew Dad would have followed and this should have made her happy. My mother's mental health was worth any inconvenience on my part, so I talked to her for about an hour. She regained her composure. Since, the event she wanted to attend was over, there was no point walking around the deck once we finished talking. I felt she had accepted the situation and would be okay.

In the interim, Dad wandered the ship alone. He tried to find the cabin and kept walking around the deck, not knowing his room number. Thankfully, I found him on the same deck as our cabin. He must have walked around and around not seeing anything that was familiar to him. I felt bad, but he seemed to be in good humor about what had happened. Although, he knew something was terribly wrong, it was not until I got him into the cabin that we sat and talked. Dad listened as I explained to him why Mother was upset. Finally, Mother showed up. She and Dad reunited, without a major incident.

I went up to the upper deck where Carrie said she would be and found her listening to a band that kept playing the same song over and over again. I think it was the only one that they knew. Carrie walked away from the performance and to this day she detests that song. It is hard for me to "stomach" that tune as well.

On the cruise, we often dressed for dinner. Whether we were attending an informal or formal meal, Dad, Mother, Carrie and I always got ready for dinner as if it was a special occasion. The service for the formal dinners took a little longer. We had the same head waiter and he always provided us with a good time as we either waited for dinner or he offered his opinion on what meal to select. The waiter was from Singapore and the assistant waiter was from Ghana.

During one meal, Dad sat next to a fellow from

Lake City. Both men were veterans and had a great deal in common. They talked for the hour nonstop, comparing notes on WWII, military service, places in Lake City, Seattle, the Lake Forest Park government matters and many other topics. I was impressed because I knew Dad struggled to remember some things and had a difficult time during the conversation. However, he was his old self and carried on throughout the evening like a trooper. After the meal, he commented about how much he missed a good conversation and how good it felt to express himself as he did aptly, prior to the dementia. I reflected on the time that I had spent with my father and felt I needed to give him other opportunities to express himself in a similar way in other settings. Unfortunately, those moments were now few and far between.

When we arrived in Acapulco, the temperature rose to over 80 degrees and we enjoyed our stay on this warm day that in more northern climates would be rather chilly. This was a refreshing change from the cold weather we usually experienced. As a result, we saw the city in all its glory by walking or catching a cab from one end of the city to the other. The cabs seemed to be small

German-made cars.

So, Mother and Dad took a formal bus tour while Carrie and I took a cab going in a different direction. Mother and Dad wanted to see The Ecumenical Chapel of Peace and other sites identified on their tour. Carrie and I asked the cab driver to take us all over Acapulco and show us the sites. The driver was knowledgeable and spoke great English. He explained to us that he had stayed in the Midwest for a while and returned to Acapulco to work "with the tourist crowd." He drove us by the Ecumenical Chapel of Peace as well as other highlights of the city.

Finally, he drove us to the famed La Quebrada Cliffs. We saw brave men and sometimes women divers climb high onto the cliffs and then they took a plunge into the warm clear water below. One wondered, if they were able to make the perfect dive every time because of the narrow inlet they dived into. One false move may have spelled tragedy. But, the experienced divers attracted tourists from all over the world to watch. Carrie and I were enthralled and we stayed quite a while. Meanwhile, Dad and Mother's tour was over and we ended up in the same location. What a wonderful coincidence to cap off our Acapulco adventure. Also, one of the young divers impressed Mother so much, that she kept talking about him, and described how kind and courteous he was to her. This is because when he emerged from his dive and was out of the water he walked passed my mother. He smiled at her and offered a friendly greeting. I think she was smitten. Carrie and I laughed at the thought.

All four of us boarded the cruise ship again for a long ride back up the Rivera. The cruise-line staff had planned one last port-of-call, but it had to be cancelled because one of the ship's engines cut out and they could not fix it until we docked in San Diego. The cruise officials offered us some amenities, but they were small and did not really satisfy the passengers. Generally speaking, it was a successful and enjoyable trip. However, Mom, Dad, Carrie and I looked forward to returning to the U.S. We arrived in San Diego, disembarked and were happy except for our trying experience just prior to arriving in Acapulco, where Mother missed her program.

FAILING MEMORY

Dad appeared to have managed his dementia reasonably well at this point, but we needed to be with him at all times.

Larry Calkins

CHAPTER 15 – ADULT DAY CENTER

It must have been in the early spring of 2001, when I came to Lake Forest Park for a weekend as I often did, during this period of time. I drove from Bend, Oregon. It was a long five hour haul and I called Mother as we passed Issaquah which was located at the base of Snoqualmie Pass. I told her I planned to drop Carrie off at my brother-in-law's house and then I would be on my way north. I planned to call Mother again when I left Renton.

As I dropped Carrie off, my anxiety kicked in because I intuitively felt something was wrong. We arrived at Carrie's brother's house in Renton, sat in his living room briefly, and had a polite conversation with Pete and Joan, Carrie's brother and sister-in-law. Then, I explained, I needed to leave for Lake Forest Park and bid them a fond adieu.

I am not sure why I became anxious to leave. Somehow I felt an urgency to make the most of my time with Dad in Lake Forest Park. At the time, I knew Dad was not problem solving well and often forgot many important things. Besides, I wanted to gain as much insight into his background as I could before he completely lost his ability to recall information.

After I called Mother, letting her know my ETA, I left Renton and began my trek up I-405 to Lake Forest Park which was about 30 minutes from where I was driving. Several moments before I called Mother, she must have suggested to Dad, "Go downstairs and make Larry's bed, so he has a comfortable place to stay when he arrives."

So, I traveled quickly to Lake Forest Park to begin my weekend with my parents. The highway was teaming with vehicles, but the trip to Bothell remained rather fast at freeway speed. I turned and traveled through Bothell; heading on to Lake Forest Park.

After leaving the city of Bothell and nearing Lake Forest Park city limits, I came around a large bend in the narrow roadway known to locals as "dead man's" corner. I saw a man walking briskly along the highway. I looked closer and thought it may be my father. Initially, I did not believe it was him and thought I must have been mistaken.

I surmised that this must have been a stranded motorist or someone who lived nearby because of the clothes he was wearing. He did not look like he was dressed for a walk in this cold weather "let alone" a brisk hike. The man had on a plaid sleeveless sweater, khaki pants and dress shoes. As I drove by, I thought, "I'll never forgive myself, nor will Mother, if I keep driving and the man that I passed really is my father." Further, I reasoned that if he was Dad, and reached Bothell, there was no way I could find him, because I would not know which direction he may decide to take as he continued to walk. I knew there was a possibility that Dad might not stop or turn around until he became confused. It was imperative for me to find answers to the questions that were "racing" in my head. So, I turned my car around and went back to check.

I took the next left and essentially made a U-turn to get back to where I had seen the man. I saw him again and became convinced that it was Dad. I turned into a fruit stand that was on the other side of dead-man's corner and pulled a quick K turn to head back toward him as he walked toward me. Because the roadway was narrow, I pulled over into a driveway that went up a hill, stopped the car, got out and walked toward him.

When I was close enough to him, I said, "Dad, what are you doing on this highway?" He appeared to be in a very happy and jovial mood. Endorphins must have been surging through his body from all the brisk walking.

He stopped and looked at me incredulously, and replied, "Why coming to meet you, of course."

I said, "Well, am I glad to see you." I wondered if he would have walked to Oregon to see me.

He smiled and replied, "I am glad to see you too." He knew his hike was over and his mission fulfilled.

We walked back to the car, and I said, "I bet there is someone who is wondering where you are." I whipped my cell phone out from my pocket and said, "Do you want to talk to her?"

He responded with the marvel of wonder like a small child seeing an object for the first time, "On that?"

pointing to the cell phone.

I said, "Yes" and I dialed Mother. When Mom answered, I said, "I think someone wants to talk to you." As I handed him the device, Dad did not miss a beat and talked to her just like he was in the house safe and sound. Dad gave me back the phone and I explained that I had found Dad wondering down Bothell Way and I was bringing him home. Mother had no idea that Dad had left the house. I was grateful that I stopped and we could be reunited again.

Afterwards, I pieced things together. I figured out that Dad must have walked down the stairs at the house and left by using the backdoor. He headed off from the house, walking toward Bothell to find me. That meant he had traveled about 4 miles (about an hour and 20 minute walk) on foot.

***

Generally, Mother kept up her spirits but the responsibility of caring for Dad on an ongoing basis weighed on her, heavily. She placed Dad in adult day care program which was part of a local senior suite of programs for patients with dementia to relieve caregivers who needed a respite during the day. Intuitively, Dad knew that Mother needed relief. Joyfully and honorably, he agreed to go to the day care program for several hours to give "Mother a break."

Another senior program provided a basic transportation need within the Lake Forest Park and Bothell communities. When called upon with a 24 hour notice, a wheelchair access mini-bus would stop in front of the house, pick up a client, transport them to medical appointments, shopping trips, the adult day center and other locations. Mother worked with the local senior programs and knew about those services.

Consequently, Dad smiled at the driver as he walked up the steps to the waiting doors of the mini-bus which took him to the day center. He told me they drove him all over creation in order to pick up others and deliver them to their destination.

One day, while I was visiting Dad and Mother, she suggested that I should go to the day center and get Dad. Mother told me she would call and cancel his appointment with the mini-van that was scheduled to bring him home. She suggested that I stay for about an hour with Dad, see what took place and I could bring him home. Gladly, I drove to the center.

I am not sure what I expected, but I did not anticipate participating in anything; just observing. When I arrived, Dad was overjoyed and happily welcomed me. We sat in a circle and sang songs. These were songs Dad knew well and he did not need to look at the words. I on the other hand, kept my copy of the music and hoped I would not stand out as I tried to sing along. Dad and I played games with the other seniors. These were simple almost childlike games, such as bouncing a large ball to one another in a circle and the hokey pokey that would challenge their dexterity and mental capabilities.

I must express a feeling of pride for my father for his ability to see the day care center as a place where it was necessary for him to be at that time. I believe he learned how to cope with his disease and remain calm through difficult situations. Whether it was intuitive or not, Dad knew whatever help the day center provided was important for his well-being. Simply speaking, when he was at the center Mother had a break from caring for him.

Dad and the other men joked that they were inmates at the day center. They felt confined to perform activities that were often stilted and juvenile. Their daily routine may have turned into moments filled with expressions of sadness or even bitterness that normally did not last too long.

Whatever Dad and these men thought, they were determined to make the best of their situation. They complied with the requirements of making the journey from the house to the adult center and back safely again without disruption.

Dad kept a notebook and a memory journal. I never saw him write anything in his notebook while I was there. Yet, he kept his notebook handy just in case it was needed. Often, he wrote notes at home to remind himself of things he wanted to remember

My father became a new type of man and I decided I needed to view him as he is now and not as he had been in the past. Although, I was left with the void of knowing

I would never see the "old form" of Dad again. I focused on moving forward in a new direction.

When we returned home from the day center, Dad and I continued to talk and I helped him where I could around the house. Mother remained in bed during the early afternoon, trying to get some rest. I did not think much about it, but Dad off-handedly stated, "She seems to be in bed a lot nowadays." His words surprised and impacted me. I began to realize that her normal disposition had changed and was likely due to the strain of being Dad's caregiver.

Finally, Mother awoke and said to Dad, "Travis why don't you take Larry out to the garage and help him clean it up?" I was a little startled and I started to question her by asking what exactly she wanted done in the garage. Dad said, "That's okay, I know what to do." Evidently, she had made similar statements to him several times.

So, Dad and I dutifully went to the garage to clean as well as sort items. Initially, taking my father's lead, I started putting things into buckets and containers. As we talked, Dad agreed that some of the things he would never use again. Those items could go to a second hand store or other charities. We enjoyed talking and being in each other's company with a purpose of getting the garage cleaned. We spent a couple of hours at the task and I felt a sense of accomplishment afterwards.

Later that year, caring for Dad became enough of a stress for Mother that she needed not only daytime relief but also longer terms of respite. She contacted the Veteran's Administration and decided to place Dad in the veteran's home for those with dementia near Fort Lewis in Tacoma. She discussed with Dad what she wanted to do and he agreed with her. My father enjoyed getting out and meeting new people. He knew deep down inside that Mother must have some time away from him.

The Veteran's Affairs Medical Center near Tacoma offered Dad accommodations for up to a two week stay. I found out about his stay at the Center from my brother. While I was sure about the good quality of care Dad would receive, I wished mom had discussed it with me.

FAILING MEMORY

The State of Oregon provided me with generous benefits working as an Enviromental Specialist with plenty of sick leave and vacation time. I decided that I could take some time to be a caregiver for my father. Therefore, after he was discharged from the VA Center, I proposed an alternative method of taking care of Dad to Mother. Periodically, I would take Dad for a week or two to give him the care that he needed and Mother a rest. *This proved to be one of the most rewarding experiences I had with my father.*

Larry Calkins

CHAPTER 16 – VISITS TO BEND AND THE DALLES

Dad seemed happy to comply with the arrangement that Mother and I made about his visits with me. I would leave for Seattle, pick him up and bring my father to Bend, Oregon on a regular basis. This occurred about once every three to six months. Often, I would travel to Lake Forest Park on the weekend, pick up Dad and take him back the next weekend or the following one. It depended on the length of his stay.

Hettie, my daughter, and Brian, my son-in-law, moved to Eureka, California. Hettie, Carrie and I discussed taking a trip to Cave Junction to look at the Oregon Caves. We were trying to find a place in-between Bend and Eureka to visit as well as enjoy each other's company. Dad happened to be with us that week and the three of us packed for the trip to meet Hettie, Brian and a friend in Grants Pass, Oregon. In Grants Pass, we stayed at a hotel with 3 rooms. Hettie and Brian's friend agreed to have Dad stay with him. At the last minute, Carrie felt uncomfortable with the arrangement because she expected Dad to be disoriented, not knowing his roommate and potentially react poorly. Wisely, Carrie said, "What if your father has a concern and needs comfort?" I said, "We would be right down the hall." That did not satisfy her. She said, "I would feel more comfortable if he stayed with us." So, Dad slept in the bed on one side of the room and we felt comfortable being in the bed a few feet from him.

We fell asleep quickly. When I woke about 2 a.m. Dad was looking out the window with a puzzled look on his face. I said "Dad, you look perplexed."

He said, "I am—where am I?"

In a reassuring voice I said, "We are in Grants Pass at a hotel and are planning on going to the Oregon Caves tomorrow." He said, "Oh, Okay" and went back to bed. It bothered me that he did not remember the discussion we had planning our itinerary the day before this incident occurred. I was beginning to see a pattern. I remembered Grandmother's fears. I did not want Dad to wake a few minutes later and repeat the scenario, so I stayed awake the rest of the night. If it was necessary, I could quickly reassure him again. He never woke until morning.

The next morning when we awoke, everyone was refreshed except for me. I needed a cup of coffee. We found Hettie, Brian and their friend already at breakfast. Dad and I wandered in and I helped Dad obtain his breakfast at the buffet the hotel offered. Dad joined in on the morning conversation, asking how we all slept. He never mentioned his night's sleep. Without his prompting, again I gently reminded him of the day's itinerary and he became eager to see the Oregon Caves. We all piled into our cars and in a little over an hour we arrived at the Oregon Caves National Monument. We signed up for a tour and at the appropriate time were escorted through the entrance. Dad and I picked up the rear of our party. I made sure Dad ducked as he approached a short entryway. He took things in stride and walked carefully as we marveled at the stalagmites and stalactites throughout the cave.

The uneventful, but memorable event, allowed Dad's reactions to be appropriate all the way through the experience. Adeptly, he hid any memory loss or problem solving difficulties. I allowed him to use me as a crutch, ask his questions and be quiet when he felt the need not to say anything. Dad enjoyed talking immensely to Hettie and Brian's friend from Eureka, but never really got into great depth with his conversation. Brian's friend commented to me that he did not see signs of dementia and felt that Dad was a regular guy. By this time, Dad was proficient at covering up any of his misgivings and was able to operate on autopilot during conversations. He relied on past memories and would recall them when it was necessary. He had an exceptionally good day.

Carrie and Hettie commented to one another that Dad appeared very happy and interested in the caves. He smiled, talked, asked questions and seemed to thoroughly enjoy himself. Hettie and Carrie lamented the fact that most likely he would not remember the experience tomorrow, but for now his emotional responses remained high and no one regretted bringing him along.

That afternoon, we parted from Hettie, Brian and friend. Happily Dad, Carrie and I drove back to Bend late that evening.

FAILING MEMORY

Later that week, Dad and I discovered the Bend Lava Caves. We walked through from one end to another and then walked the trails on top of the lava beds near the caves. Dad appeared to enjoy his experience with nature but persisted being less talkative than he had been days before our time together. I was not exactly sure what to think, even after asking him, "Dad, what are you thinking about?" Also, we walked through Sun River, which is a small tourist community near Bend. Dad became a little more talkative as we drove through the community that was constructed of streets with endless round-a-bouts at every block. We were headed home.

***

I enjoyed cooking for Dad. In the morning I would wake, go downstairs, start fixing oatmeal, or eggs and bacon and on occasion pancakes. When Dad awoke, he dressed himself and came down the short flight of stairs to the dining area. It never failed; he would ask his first question of the day, "How did you sleep last night?" I answered him and then I asked him about yesterday's events. Often, he did not recall the events. Surprised, I would conduct additional query. He would ask the same questions he asked the day before and I would give him similar answers to his questions each time. This bothered me, because my encounters with Dad reminded me of a popular movie. Every day's events repeated the previous day with minor variations. Although, I tried to vary his activities, it did not seem to matter. The conversation always began the same and I provided similar responses.

***

I knew we needed to spice things up a little. He loved playing golf. I did not care how I entertained my father, as long as we were together and cheerfully he enjoyed himself. I knew of a golf course with long fairways, a few water hazards and fewer golfers on the weekdays. I drove us to Prineville, which is about 30 miles from our home in Bend. The short trip took us through some pretty juniper country. One Prineville council member described the golf course to me as a disguised sewage treatment plant.

Previously, the City of Prineville violated waste water regulations with effluent discharging or the outflowing of contaminated water into the Crooked River

222

from the city's sewage treatment plant. To remedy the violations, Prineville elected to create water hazards with the effluent discharge into ponds at the golf course. The ponds polished the effluent by any remaining bacteria eating residual sewage before the effluent entered the groundwater and eventually reentered the Crooked River. Additionally, microbial action in the soil purifies the effluent. The effluent also helped irrigate the golf course, keeping the grass green without fertilizer. The innovative fix allowed Prineville to solve a problem and even allowed the city to earn a modest income from tourists looking for a golfing experience.

As I explained how the golf course worked to Dad, his interest peaked, but obviously he really anticipated the golfing encounter. To begin, we arrived at the clubhouse, talked to the city employee and rented golf clubs. A smile returned to my father's face. He developed a banter about golf, golfing friends, family, past and present relatives.

Dad had cataracts in both eyes which caused him to have a cloudy visual experience. He wore glasses, but they hung around his neck with a retainer strap. It did not matter that he never looked through his glasses, as he enjoyed himself playing golf. He would ask me, "Larry can you point to the pin? Show me where it is." Dutifully, I would point, he would look down my arm at the pin, take his stance and hit the ball. Invariably, it would go straight and surprisingly toward the pin. I would take my swing and sometimes the ball went straight but more often than not, I would slice it to the left or right. Therefore, the ball would go into the rough. I racked up points. Dad kept his to a minimum. We would laugh and talk about the shots. I did not care that my points mounted up twice as high on the score card as Dad's. I would not have traded these moments for anything in my life. More than playing golf, I enjoyed being with my father.

In a way, my father became a new form of himself, but at the same time he was the same person. I reacted and interacted with him much differently than I had a few years earlier. He depended on me. Still, he became my friend and partner. I took the time and "smelled the roses" to experience my father like I had never experienced him before!

FAILING MEMORY

***

On one of Dad's visits, I decided to help Hettie by driving her over packed car from mid-southern Oregon to Bend. My son-in-law, Brian found a new job at a University in eastern Washington and went there to start working. He left his job at a mill in Eureka, CA. Brian rented a large truck to move most of their belongings and Hettie stayed behind in Eureka to finish packing any remaining items. This included packing her car so she could barely see out the back. She planned to stop, leave much of the "stuff" from her car at our house, and return to Bend to collect her belongings at a later date.

Game for something new, Dad agreed to go with me to rescue Hettie's over packed car. Hettie was determined to make "great" time in her travel to meet us. Therefore, we kept in touch by cell phone.

On the way, I suggested to Dad that he drive. Dad declined, stating he did not feel confident in his abilities to drive anymore. Content, he accepted riding in the passenger seat and going along with me.

We met Hettie at the entrance to Crater Lake; she

was dog-tired. Hettie agreed to drive my car and I would drive hers the rest of the way to Bend. Dad agreed to keep her company. I hoped that he and she would develop an enriched grandfather to granddaughter rapport on the way. While they did, the trip to Bend for me went quickly and terminated with me being fatigued from the long drive. Hettie flopped on the bed exhausted when she arrived in Bend.

***

During that visit and future visits, I noticed Dad continued not to remember activities that happened the previous day. It scared me a little, because I hoped he would have stories to tell Mother when he returned from his visit to our home. I continued to develop daily activities with fun-filled things to do, in order to keep Dad's mind active. I began to realize that often he would just follow instructions and do what others thought he should do.

On other trips, when Dad came to Bend, in order to give Mother a respite from caring for him, I took him golfing again. Also, we explored quite a few places that included Santiam Pass, Paulina Peak, Paulina Lake, East Lake, the Newberry Crater and Big Obsidian Flow. We took the elevated Cascades Highway and our canoe out on Sparks and Elk Lakes.

One weekend, Emma came home from college. We decided to go to Sparks Lake and take the canoe. The lake exhibited low water that summer and we carefully maneuvered our canoe out through the boulders onto the lake proper. Dad sat on a pad in the middle with a paddle with Emma up front and me in the back. Dad insisted on paddling, but I wanted to steer the boat. Emma was an experienced rower. She learned this skill when she attended church summer camps.

I dropped Emma off on a far shore with Dad and she entertained him while I rowed back to the car to pick up Carrie. It was not very efficient, but I sat in the back as I always did trying to steer and paddle. Instead of rowing from the middle of the canoe to balance my weight, the front end of the boat went up in the air and I had little control. It remained a wonder that I did not capsize the boat. Still I persevered; finally made it back to the far shore where Emma and Dad were waiting.

When we arrived, I apologized for taking so long, but Dad as always with good humor said, "That's alright, Emma and I talked about the price of tea in China and we figured things out." Carrie and Emma decided to hike back on the trail. Dad, Carrie and Emma did not know that I was still mortified from my experience.

Dad and I piled into the canoe and paddled back to the starting point. Dad was sitting in the front of the boat and he became very uncomfortable. I pulled over to the shore where I knew there was another trail back to the car. Dad got out of the boat, while I paddled back to the beginning of our trip. I had much better experiences with my father in Bend than that day on Sparks Lake. When we arrived home he expressed he was happy to be back and out of the canoe.

When it came time to take Dad back to Seattle, we decided it would be a good experience for him to take the train from Portland to Seattle. I made arrangements for Mother to pick up Dad at the King Street Train Station in Seattle. Mother agreed and we drove Dad to Portland to catch the train. I did not think much about it until we got to the train station. I planned to purchase the tickets for him and the ticketing official asked for his ID. Of course, I had my identification but they wanted Dad's as he was the traveler. Without realizing it, I had left his wallet on the dresser in our house. The ticket agent took it upon himself to lambast Dad for not having his ID. I tried to explain that it was my fault, but that did not matter. The ticket master wanted to get something off of his chest. He stated, "Do you remember a thing called 9-11 (of course Dad did not), and we need to know all of our passengers. Without identification we cannot tell who is who. You could be a terrorist for all we know."

My imagination escalated, thinking of Dad as a terrorist. It seemed ridiculous to consider him a terrorist or someone who could plot anything. Obviously, he was a threat to no one.

Dad stood there, not saying a word and accepted the humiliating rebuff from this man. Finally, I had enough. Abruptly, I told the agent we would not be using the train. Instead, we would be driving Dad to Seattle and there was no need for his services. I told Dad not to worry. I would get him home safely. I called Mother letting her know the change in plans.

I was concerned about the obvious. First, the ticket agent had no reason to admonish Dad the way he did. Second, I became increasingly concerned about Dad's safety boarding the train by himself. How would others on the train treat Dad? Would he be treated courteously, ignored or worse, be further humiliated? I was not going to find out. We left by car for Seattle.

***

In December 2002, we moved to The Dalles which is north of Bend to be closer to Mother and Dad. I continued to bring Dad to our home and explore the area. I drove him to The Dalles, telling him we were driving down the east side of the Cascade Mountains. As a curiosity, when we got to the Columbia River I asked him which direction he thought we should take in order to go along the river. He said, "Take a right when you cross the river." His uncanny sense of direction thrilled me. I do not know if he just guessed or if he truly knew to turn right and go west. If we were to travel to Pendleton, what would he have said? Would he say. "Left to the east?" I'll never know. We turned right and travelled the short 20 miles to The Dalles. I drove up to our new home and we walked inside.

While sitting in the living room, Dad and I began chatting. I asked him what he thought of the house. He said the living room looked "commodious." I did not know what the word meant. Here's a guy theoretically suffering from dementia and he spit out the word commodious like a Rhodes Scholar. After WWII he did attend Oxford[1] for a short while but I do not think that is where the word came from. I think in the recesses of his mind he used the word and it fit. I asked him what the word meant. He said "large, roomy and comfortable." Yep, the room looked large. We placed our furniture in a way that conversation could easily take place and at the same time you could look out through a sliding glass door with picture windows, peering over the deck and beyond to the Columbia River. A commodious room fit nicely the description of the space.

That evening, Carrie and I gave Dad our bedroom so he could be comfortable and we took the bedroom across the hall. Our dog, Nala, quietly went about her

---

[1] While in the Army Air Corps, he was assigned to attend Oxford while he was stationed in England for additional pilot training.

business in the house and mostly stayed out of the way or out of sight. Late that night, Dad woke up. I thought it might be a repeat of the Grants Pass experience where he did not know where he was. As he walked by our room, I asked him, "Dad can I help you? Is there something you need?"

He responded very agitated and said, "No, I can't find what I'm looking for."

I asked him, "What are you looking for?"

In a loud voice he said, "I don't know. I can't find it."

Carrie said, "You're scaring the dog." Meanwhile, Nala had scooted down deep under the bed to hide.

Dad said, "I don't want a dog here. You need to get rid of the dog."

Carrie said, "Do you see a dog? The dog is gone."

I said, "Dad why don't you go back to bed. We'll find whatever you are looking for in the morning."

Finally, Dad calmed down. He remained agitated, but could not argue. He did not have the strength. I said,

"Your bed is in here and if you want to look at the river you can look out this window." I pointed to the narrow window at the top of the room and showed him the panoramic view of the river. Dad stood looking out the window. Most likely, he did not remember the commodious living room or where he was; scaring him further. Somehow, we got Dad back to bed and he awoke the next morning his cheery self, yet he was still contemplative.

When I considered this experience, I was too tired to think clearly when I talked with Dad that night. Whenever Dad and I talked, I tried different forms and methods of reasoning with him but this time his agitation got worse.

Oddly, Dad loved dogs. As a kid, he owned many dogs and his parents had dogs until they passed away. It was not until late in his life that he and Mother owned cats and no dogs. Perhaps, he did not remember owning the animals. Later in life his intolerance of dogs became a symptom of his dementia.

The day we got ready to leave to take Dad back

home to Seattle, he and I shuffled around doing menial tasks and tried to fill the time before we departed. A little while later, Carrie had a problem with the computer and needed my help. All of a sudden, I heard the front door close. Dad had walked out. We lived at the top of a hill on a dead end street with only one way to go which was down the hill and to the left. Any other way he walked would have led him to a dead end road, the hospital or back to our house. I helped Carrie with the computer and finally said, "Dad walked out of the house. I need to go find him." She agreed and let me go while she finished her work.

I ran down the hill until I could see him walking toward the bottom where he would either turn left or right. I called after him. He kept walking. I caught up with him and talked in a convincing manner so that he would go back to the house. He did so reluctantly, but complied. Finally, it was time for us to go and Dad's cheerful disposition returned. We left for Seattle.

***

In the spring of 2003, Emma graduated from the

University of Puget Sound (UPS) in Tacoma. We left for Emma's graduation. Carrie and I left The Dalles for Tacoma and my brother Steve, Mother and Dad came down to Tacoma from Seattle for the event. Carrie's Mother and her husband, and her father, Richard, also came to the graduation. Carrie's Dad's spouse had passed the previous summer. Emma's fiancé, Jason, also attended with his parents. Jason met Emma at UPS and he had graduated from the school a year earlier and left for Mesa, Arizona to start a career. He and Emma planned to live there after she graduated. He returned for Emma's graduation.

The graduation was held in the University's stadium. The extended family wore heavy coats and snuggled together in the bleachers as we squinted to see the graduating seniors. Emma walked up, collected her diploma and we could barely make out where she was as she crossed the stage. Afterward, we took pictures and joined in on the merriment at the University. Dad was sociable as he joined in the photo opportunities by standing next to the graduate.

A couple of weeks later, Jason and Emma planned

their wedding in Tacoma. Dad, Mother and Steve again returned to Tacoma for the nuptials. Just prior to the actual ceremony, our son-in-law, Brian, escorted Mother down the aisle with Dad walking fairly close behind. I could tell, Dad's confidence waned as he shuffled behind Brian and Mother. Dad sat with the other extended family guests near the front as Reverend Anthony Phinney, performed the wedding ceremony. Quiet and unassuming, Dad took in the celebration and even danced with Mother in a sweet fashionable way as their humanity, on the dance floor, swayed to the music.

The following day, Emma and Jason left for Mesa, Arizona with Jason's parents driving a trailer load of Emma's belongings. They were traveling south and stopped briefly by The Dalles to gather a few additional possessions she had stored at our house.

***

On another summer visit to The Dalles, Mother decided to come and pick Dad up. She spent an evening at The Dalles enjoying time with us. On the way back, Dad, Mother and I stopped along the Columbia River to watch the wind surfers as they went back and forth across the river. We felt like recreationers sitting amongst those folks who were sunning themselves on the beach alongside their boards. It was a pleasant afternoon. We bid goodbye at the surfer site. Mother and Dad left for Lake Forest Park and I drove to The Dalles.

Larry Calkins

CHAPTER 17 – MEMORY CARE FACILITIES

As the primary care giver for Dad, Mother needed to make decisions for his wellbeing, listen to him and accommodate his desires. This was a tall order for which she had no formal training. However, instinctively she knew what Dad wanted and in her quiet way went about addressing his concerns. It was paramount for Mother to consider Dad's medical welfare and safety because at this point in time she could not continue to be his care giver. Dad's daily needs were too overwhelming for her to handle.

In September 2004, Mother made the decision to place Dad in a memory care facility. She chose a facility that was located near Lake Forest Park. This place was a relatively modern, pleasant, brightly lighted residence that was under new management. The building was outfitted with staff that were trained to care for Alzheimer's patients.

A small lobby outside the locked unit allowed families to greet the staff and be sign-in. To enter, we were buzzed through a solid door that entered an area that reminded me of the outdoors (only it was fully enclosed indoors). Along a pathway, there were murals of trees, birds and other outdoor settings painted on the walls. A large mural covered the door we had just entered which led back to the lobby. I had to look carefully to see the latch and buzzer that would allow me or others out. As I looked forward, to one corner of the pathway, a rustic porch was constructed with a wooden bench swing. Continuing down the pathway, I walked around a patient lounge that resembled a courtyard.

At the far end of the walkway, I observed a dining room, kitchen and recreation gathering area for the residents. On the outside of the initial building were constructed two dorm-style wings spreading out in both directions. Walking down the hallway in the dorm-style wings, the resident quarters and bathrooms were located on either side of the wing.

Dad's cozy room was located in the first wing. His room held a single bed, night stand, a chair and clothes closet. The stark setting held the essentials that provided Dad with his basic needs.

FAILING MEMORY

When I visited Dad, I noticed he had placed his comb and notebook on the night stand. He could watch TV on a small set that was located on his dresser and his clothes were placed neatly in the small closet. I am sure all of his possessions could have been placed in a large box for the move into the facility. Dad must have felt that he had reverted to his time in the military because he was currently living in crisp new surroundings. I surmised, that unlike military personnel, the staff at the residence made him feel comfortable and relaxed.

As we sat on Dad's bed talking, a neighbor from two doors down came to visit us. The visitor introduced himself and Dad made polite conversation with him. Our guest picked up Dad's comb and began combing his hair. Dad did not notice and continued to talk to the man. He responded naturally, as if the man had brought his own comb with him. When the man left, he slipped Dad's comb into his pocket and left the room. I thought of telling a staff member about it but figured Dad may go to the man's room and use his comb there, so I did not bother. Dad did not care.

The day I arrived at this memory care facility, Dad

showed me around. He liked to walk around the courtyard. According to him, he was often joined by other residents on his walks. However, that day it was just the two of us. We circled on the pathway, walking and talking. When we became tired, he and I sat in the little alcove and continued to talk.

A little while later, the caregiver announced that the singing group Dad normally participated in was scheduled to meet in about 5 minutes. I said, "I'd like to sit in."

Dad was excited that I wanted to sing with him and his group.

Proudly, Dad walked with me to the place where we would be singing. He and I were the first ones to arrive. I noticed, the chairs were arranged in a circle and one of the leaders had placed song books on the seats of each chair. The song books were written in large print that appealed to the elderly residents.

As the other residents came into the room, a young lady, who was a little older than me wanted the chair I was sitting in. I was sitting next to Dad on his right side.

Evidently, she preferred that side of him as well. I suggested that she sit in the empty chair on Dad's left and she complied. I was still a little unnerved as I watched how she carefully interacted with Dad. I found out, that she and Dad enjoyed each other's company on more than one occasion. She flirted with him and kept him entertained, when I could not during the singing session. Obviously, he appreciated her comradery.

Dad's cataracts clouded his vision and he had glasses that hung around his neck so they could be easily placed over his eyes, but he rarely used them. He knew the words to most of the songs anyway and did not need the books. When he was asked to sing a song that he was not familiar to him, he simply hummed along with the music. When Dad sang it was in harmony. His tenor voice blended well with the other singers. I am not sure where he learned to sing perfect harmony or if he just faked it, but he always sang in key and I loved listening to him. I was not as talented as Dad and I simply sang the melody. Still, both of us sounded pretty good singing together and often we carried the tune for the rest of the group.

After the singing event, one of the caregivers came up to me afterward and acknowledged that Dad and this lady who was younger than him often talked together. She said, "I allow this to continue, but when your Mother comes, I remove the lady from your Dad's vicinity and your Mother is none the wiser." The care provider protected my mother from being jealous or humiliated.

***

In 2002, Marcella our middle daughter, left for Wisconsin to pursue a graduate degree. Before she left the west coast, she decided to visit grandparents in Seattle to say goodbye and enjoy their company. She relayed a conversation she had with my father who told her a war story. Dad explained that he would fly to various locations in France to deliver supplies to the troops who were near the front during World War II. Dad said, "We would often fly over the country trying to find a landing strip and then through the fog one would appear before we landed at the site." He hesitated for a long moment, looking like he contemplated saying something. Marcella said. "I didn't see signs of dementia. I was perplexed and continued listening for what came next." Then, Dad continued, "Somehow, we found those sites and landed safely every time."

Later, as Marcella retold the story, she wondered, "Maybe Grandpa hesitated because he thought about how his mind became foggy." Then rhetorically, she asked, "What gave him the ability to seek and to find the sites or for that matter deal with his dementia?" I did not have a good answer. Marcella asked and answered her own question, "I thought you may say—his faith in God."

In October of 2004, in Wisconsin, Marcella and her girlfriend came back to the west coast in order to hold a commitment ceremony in Medford, Oregon. We made elaborate arrangements to attend Marcella's function. Unlike our youngest daughter's wedding in Tacoma, nearly everyone needed to travel and stay overnight in Medford. I wanted my family in attendance, especially my father because now he stayed in a memory care facility. Carrie and I knew it would be difficult for Mother to care for Dad in a hotel. We confronted this dilemma by researching the owners of the memory care facility. They operated a similar unit in Medford. I inquired about an overnight stay for Dad at this facility and they were accommodating.

When we arrived at the Medford unit it was rather late. This was the night before the commitment ceremony. I made arrangements that included the time and day the staff could expect my father. Dad bounced up to the door like a kid going to a slumber party and he knocked. When the attendant opened the door, Dad walked through it and into the facility like he knew the place. I felt very comfortable leaving him there.

The next day, Mother and Dad arrived at the ceremony. Nervously, I watched Dad and tried to gauge his level of self-confidence. He seemed to respond okay, but I worried about his ability to follow directions. I assured myself that he would be in the proper place at the proper time. Brian and Jason, our sons-in-law, escorted the grandmothers to their seats. We expected Dad to follow Mother. Jason cradled Mothers arm and escorted her to her place. Like a trooper, Dad followed them at a respectful distance and did very well. All of the relatives were seated in the same area.

Dad made it through the event under Mother's

watchful eye. He held a song book steady for himself and her. Upon greeting Marcella after the ceremony Dad gave her a gentle kiss on the cheek and a larger than life smile as he congratulated his granddaughter on the accomplishment.

Mother and Dad left for Lake Forest Park after the ceremony and did not stay for the reception or a second night. Still, I was happy that my parents attended the ceremony and it turned out well.

***

One weekend after Marcella's event in Medford, I came up to Seattle to visit Dad. My brother Steve and I went without Mother to the Lake Forest Park memory care facility. We walked into the unit as normal, but Dad was not in his room. I went to the activity room and asked the caregiver, "Where is my Dad?" He did not know but said he would look for him. I did not see the caregiver again. About 10 to 15 minutes later I saw Dad. He walked toward Steve and me, down the opposite wing of the facility to the activity room where we waited. He was dressed in other people's garments that overlaid his clothes. His hair looked like it had not been combed for a while and the disheveled look helped explain his puzzled nature as he walked up to us. His eyes were downcast. Obviously, he had been caught by surprise.

I do not think Steve dared say anything provocative. He was extraordinarily quiet and followed my lead.

I am not sure Dad recognized Steve or me or possibly he wanted to avoid us altogether. It was a disconcerting moment for me and likely Steve too. I tried to accept the situation. I greeted Dad with a happy, "Hi Dad," and we began our afternoon visit together. Steve helped me escort Dad back to his room. We talked on the way but I could tell he was not interested in having a long conversation.

I suggested that we go to the park and he reluctantly agreed. I helped him change into appropriate clean clothes. We found his comb and he ran it through his hair.

As we were getting ready to leave, he moved from one foot to another like a little kid who had to go to the bathroom. So, I suggested we go to the men's room. Dad and I walked into his restroom across from his bedroom. I went to a stall and he to the urinal. I do not know what happened, but he walked out. I wondered if Dad had really felt an urge to use the toilet.

I learned from caregivers that Dad suffered from incontinence. They told me that he had relieved himself elsewhere in the facility. He could no longer manage himself and needed extra care.

As I tried to find Dad in the hallway outside the bathroom, I discovered a chair with a wet cushion and a puddle on the floor underneath the chair. I did not know the cause of the accident, but I offered to clean it up. A caregiver insisted he would take care of the situation. I thanked him and went to Dad's room where I found Steve and him waiting for me. Quietly, we left and went out for our daily adventure.

A couple of weeks later on another visit, Dad and I planned to go to a different park. On the way, I needed some personal items like deodorant, and I thought Dad might enjoy going to the store with me. The store was on the way. As we entered the store we walked down the aisle, he lagged behind. He would stop and look at an item on the shelf and thoroughly examine the article. I feared he may not replace the item where he had found it or alternatively place the piece in his pocket. I tried the best I could to encourage him to keep up with me but still he lagged behind. Although, I just wanted to obtain my merchandise, pay for it and leave, Dad continued to stop and look at things along the way. I stayed with him looking at the items too, not making much progress toward the deodorant.

Then, something unconventional even for Dad happened. He spit saliva into a corner under the endcap of one of the aisles. Initially, I thought I would ignore it but then decided to say something.

I looked at him and said, "Dad, please don't do that." Without a beat, he said, "Its okay. Nobody cares."

Dad's response was totally out of character. I did not explain that this was inappropriate behavior because I did not think he would learn from the situation.

Instead, I abandoned my search for deodorant and

simply said, "Let's go to the park."

If Dad could have witnessed this incident now from the vantage point of ten years earlier, he would have been horrified at what he did and said. I realized how much *the dementia* was stealing him from me.

Slowly, I grasped conceptually, that he had taken another step down in his mental capacities. At first, I realized that he had a hard time figuring out locations and how to get from one place to another. Also, I noticed he had a hard time solving problems. He hesitated more and he seemed confused on how to do simple tasks.

As an example, one day he could not nest grocery carts in a store. He made several attempts before my daughter, Hettie, said, "That's okay Grandpa, sometimes I have difficulty with that too," and she helped him nest the cart.

Additionally, when surroundings changed, he found it difficult to keep his moral compass. His doctor told us he suspected a TIA (Transient Ischemic Attack) or a minor stroke had occurred and each event made a significant change in his life. These steps down in his abilities could be either subtle or more pronounced.

Some days, Dad seemed to adjust just fine to his surroundings. However, on other days, he definitely was lost and not alert to his setting and the people in his life. It appeared to me that he became more self-absorbed and less concerned about others needs or their welfare.

Before, he would have displayed a feeling of guilt or his sense of duty would challenge any impropriety. Now, Dad was not aware he was creating additional work for others or behaving in a manner that did not conform to normal standards. Previously, my father maintained a strong sense of awareness about people and his impact on others. That side of him had faded and at certain times had vanished entirely. It seemed to me his condition was getting worse.

In addition, to the incontinence and disruptive behavior, the management at the memory care facility suggested to Mother that she find another place for Dad. Mother was thoughtful about the move. One day, she announced that she had found another facility that was close to her house.

FAILING MEMORY

She moved Dad to a senior living center that also had an Alzheimer's and memory care wing. I was impressed by the facility. That unit of the center was located on the first floor behind locked doors which had been updated with modern fixtures and lighting. Each individual's room was larger than the previous one, but it housed fewer residents than the other memory care facility. The large dining area included a large glass windows that looked out on a nice patio area with a garden. Dad's room had a brightly lit bathroom that was attached.

Mom suspected that Dad did not like using the bathroom at the former memory care facility due to the "closed-in" feeling he had and the poor lighting. Mom lived and shopped in the neighborhood and she could visit him frequently.

After about a month, I visited Dad a second time with Mother. The manager of the unit requested to see Mother. She and I walked into the manager's office. He sat down and explained Dad's progress. It stunned me, when he suggested that we must find another place for Dad. The manager explained that this facility was not a good fit for him. He would not put Dad out on the street. However, he needed more care than this facility could provide and suggested that we contact a nursing home or an adult family home living facility. I was distraught. Our hope that this place would have been the right one for Dad evaporated.

I walked into see Dad, who had a welcoming air about him. Mother took him down to the dining area to talk. I told mother I would get a sweater for Dad, because sometimes he became cold when he was in the dining area.

In the dining area, I found Dad and Mother. I gave Dad the comb and kept the sweater close by incase he complained or simply wanted to wear it. While Dad combed his hair, Mother said she wanted to go back and talk to the manager. I stayed with Dad and we generated a pleasant conversation about his new home, what I accomplished at work, how my siblings were doing and other topics of interest. Dad appeared to be restless and not interested in our conversation. After a short while, he did not want to engage at all. I suspected Dad had lost interest in most things and that included being with family. Although, he seemed to understand our conversation, I developed a sense that I needed to keep him entertained and sadly realized that he had taken another step down in mental awareness.

On the way out of the senior living home, I articulated my observation about Dad's downward steps and expressed my concern to Mother about him taking another step in the wrong direction if we found a third facility. Others told me, research shows changing facilities can have a dramatic effect on patients with dementia. Mother acknowledged my concern and said, "We have no choice." The health provider gave Mother a list of adult care homes and nursing facilities to review.

Mother and I took the next day and visited a number of homes trying to find a good match for Dad. It was a frustrating and troubling experience. We made the best of our time, hoping for better results. So, I came up to visit Mother the following weekend and we looked at additional homes. My mother relied on my help and as difficult as it was for me, I was happy to aid her. It was hard trying to find the best fit for Dad and helping Mother make the decision where she was going to house my father.

CHAPTER 18 – ADULT CARE HOME

My father and mother enrolled in a special medical insurance patient care program when they first moved to the Seattle Area. I was a toddler at that time. It was modeled after the European healthcare systems. The company offered an insurance plan that included its own medical providers, hospitals and pharmacies. The insurance coverage provided doctors, nurses and personnel to assist with medical concerns to keep healthcare costs low. They accepted patients through their own Medicare Advantage Program where payments were made to the parent company. This form of insurance proved to be effective and much cheaper than the traditional Medicare and supplemental programs.

As far as I know, the health care program originated in the Seattle area and merged with another organization from California several years ago. The doctors who choose work in this program or the confines of the organization made referrals to other doctors within their network. There were exceptions that occurred, but generally speaking those who used this plan accepted the diagnosis, outcomes and results. The doctors all seemed to be passionate about the ideas of providing quality care for their patients.

After conducting our exhaustive search, one weekend, Mother and I settled on an adult care home in Lake Forest Park for Dad. It was on the list of facilities that the insurance company recommended. The owner operated two houses about ½ mile up the road from where Mother lived. You could walk up the hill and knock on the door, although normally we drove the short distance. One of the homes was large and presumably housed her family and had several lady boarders who needed care around the clock. The house overlooked Lake Washington with a gorgeous view of the water and an opportunity to see sea planes land at the local air harbor. This was similar to the view from Mother's house. Another smaller home that was located on the same property, was where the owner's parents lived; a mother-in-law's house per se. Another dwelling was just up the hill and next-door. This was another adult memory care home and had a large semi-circular driveway leading to the house, with a huge fir tree between the drive and the roadway. The owner offered a room in this house to Dad, which also was a residence for a lady who had her own bedroom.

The owner, who was a nurse, worked for the company that offered the medical insurance plan and was studying to become a nurse practitioner. She hired a second nurse who also stayed in the house where Dad lived. The owner's father, a retired doctor, enjoyed a quiet life and helped his daughter when it was necessary.

Mother chose this adult care home because it offered full time nursing services. The proximity of the owner's house to the homes on the property meant she would keep close watch on my father and each resident's needs in a timely fashion. In addition, the owner hired other caregivers during the day to come in and get residents up and dressed in the morning, cook their meals, clean the house and entertain them. Since Mother's house was close to the place that was caring for Dad, she attempted a trip to see him at least once a day. They would talk and take short walks around the neighborhood. Mother could not walk far herself, so short walks were as much as she could manage. Also, she feared that he may fall and this prevented her from taking him out of the immediate surroundings. Most importantly, if something happened to Dad she would need help that the caregivers could provide.

When I came to Lake Forest Park, I made a point to spend as much time as I could with my father. Often, Carrie dropped me off and then she would travel south to see her father and siblings. Alva, my sister, and her husband, Ted, were now living in California. My brother, Steve, owned a condominium but stayed with Mother at the old homestead for much of the time. Mother appreciated the company. Steve often accompanied Mother to see Dad. She would read to him, play the organ or sing songs for entertainment. When Steve came to visit, he read to him from the Bible or wheeled him outside to walk around the neighborhood. Mike, my second brother, would visit Dad on the weekends or whenever he could find the time. Mike worked long hours on his job. When he had some free time he spent it raising his family of five children. Although, he remained busy, he always found time to visit and sing or read to

Dad.

Once again, Dad's mental capacities stepped down. During the day, caregivers would place Dad in front of a huge TV screen which he watched in the common area. If they turned on the soap operas and allowed him to watch the shows while they fixed meals or cleaned the house, Dad would become completely engrossed in the programs, take on the personality of one of the characters and start yelling at the TV. It seemed as if he embodied the personalities of the characters of the programs he watched. Evidently, the dementia allowed him to no longer feel inhibited. Mother recognized this issue and suggested that the caregivers keep Dad in his bedroom. They allowed him to watch shows on a small 13 inch TV. He could easily relate to his surroundings and realize the entertainment value of the programs without always thrusting himself into the characters.

I visited Dad once or twice a month in order to spend weekends with him. If Mother needed something I would travel to the Seattle Area and spend any necessary time with her. Since, I moved to The Dalles and later to Umatilla, driving to Lake Forest Park became a matter of a 3-4 hour road trip. I drove all over Oregon for my job; therefore this seemed like a snap and I rarely hesitated to make the trip.

I brought my guitar so that we could sing songs, work on puzzles, look at photos, read books, and anything else I could think of to entertain Dad. Also, we took walks. Dad's world had turned quite small. He had a series of medical issues that required the caregivers to monitor him on a regular basis.

Dad talked less. He could not form words and it became difficult to carry on a two way conversation with him. I assumed he comprehended what I said, but it became increasingly clear that his memory and mental abilities had faded. It became harder to spend more than a couple of hours with him. On days when it was not raining, Dad and I would walk around the block. It extended about a quarter mile to the north, then a short distance to the next road over, a quarter mile down that street to the south and then the short block back to the beginning and entrance to his adult care home. We walked slowly, observing whatever flowers we saw along the way, spotted birds in the trees, commented on the neighbor's new construction projects or obvious idiosyncrasies of each home along the way. When we arrived at a break in the trees where we could see Lake Washington, we stopped and both of us observed the boats on the water or the sea planes landing on the water and commented on their appearance.

The thing I enjoyed most about my visits with Dad, was the time we would sing songs together. Although, he did not talk much now, he would sing or hum along with me as I played the guitar. I enjoyed my one person audience because he always seemed interested and participated in the songs. When he sang, it was still in harmony as I carried the melody. He belted out the old church songs as he did when I was a kid. At first he knew many of the words, but as time went on he would just hum the harmony.

On Saturday, I would spend most of my day with him and on Sunday I would stop by in the morning for a half hour or hour to sing. Depending on how I felt, we would sing older folk songs.

When I was a child, about 1959, Dad preformed in

a community play where he was the lead character. In the play his character wanted to propose to his girlfriend whose name was Daisy. Then, he kissed her on stage, asked her to marry him and sang a song.

I sung one of his favorite songs from the play with him all these years later. We laughed when we finished singing. I do not know if he remembered the play or not, but I did and that was all that mattered to me.

As the months went by, Dad's mental aptitude took more steps downward. In 2006, Mother, Steve and I took Dad to see his doctor who specialized in geriatric care. He had seen Dad since about 1997 when he first was diagnosed with vascular dementia. Dad declined to the point where he did not talk and we knew he needed additional help. Also, he stopped singing, but still hummed. Mom called him the "big hummer." Dad had been taking medicine for memory maintenance, but his outbursts at the TV and his demonstration of other signs of agitation seemed to be cause for concern and let us know the medicine might not be working. The doctor told Mother and me that we just needed to look at my father and determine the best course of action for him, because he could not tell us. The doctor prescribed medicine that was supposed to stabilize the changes in Dad's moody behavior and limit any outbursts. That did not work well because he became clumsy and could not walk. Then, the doctor prescribed medicine that was designed to calm Dad's nerves and another to help with potential depression. Finally, through the use of different medicines, as well as trial and error, Dad's irrational behavior along with his outbursts subsided.

Since, the medications helped to stabilize Dad's behavior, his reactions and interactions with family and medical staff seemed better.

In the interim, as the doctor adjusted Dad's medications, the nursing staff at the owner's adult care home gave him a wheelchair and we purchased a lift. This device helped to get Dad in and out of bed, as well as his wheelchair with ease. The owner, who by now received her nurse practitioner license, talked to us about having Dad walk again. She knew that if he stayed in the wheelchair too long, he would never walk because frankly speaking, he would forget how to walk.

So, Mom, Steve and I and many times Mike, would follow the physical therapist's recommendations, by having Dad practice walking again. Dad walked up and down the hallway at the care home when two people helped him. One of us would encourage Dad to stand and walk along beside him. It was necessary to hold on to Dad by the belt that was around his waist. The other person followed behind with the wheelchair so that if he got tired he could sit down immediately. I helped every time I came to visit, but on most occasions Steve and Mom or Steve and the caregiver, or the caregiver and Mom would help Dad walk. We tried for several months, but eventually it became onerous for anyone of us to help Dad walk. Eventually, he did not want to try, and we gave up. Dad never walked again.

The medications that finally stabilized Dad's moods and gave him the ability to function, were mixed by the staff in some pudding and placed on a spoon. Dad would take the spoon, carefully turn it around, look at it, then turn it upside down, right-side up and eventually put it in his mouth to sample the medicine infused pudding. I was amazed to see the pudding stay on the spoon as he twirled it slowly, like it was a lollipop. He wanted to see all sides before placing it in his mouth.

For the most part, the caregivers fed Dad Asian dishes. The majority of the staff were from the Philippines. That was the owner's family's origin. Dad liked different foods and never complained. Graciously, he accepted the meals and ate whatever the caregivers placed in front of him. However, he ate less now, and it was unclear to me whether he was tired of the food or simply was not hungry. Slowly, his weight decreased.

One day, Mother told me, "I know he is declining and I see his deterioration daily. I have conversations with God about what to do. I don't like to see him suffer like this." In her own way, she told me she had been thinking about Dad and wondering when...

In 2008, Dad stopped humming altogether. He barely made a sound and became less and less aware of his surroundings. When I visited, I still took him for walks, but during these times I walked by pushing him around the block in his wheelchair. We talked about the same things, but I did all the talking. He was silent, but in his silence he still had his moments of awareness. The owner had an organ in the house and Mother sat at the organ and played songs; mainly hymns, while Dad simply listen. Mom played for hours and in her quiet way communed with my father.

When I discussed my father's situation with friends or relatives, they questioned me and asked, "Does your father know who you are?" The question surprised me, and my response came naturally, "It doesn't matter to me. What I am sure of, is that my father knows I am there and that I love him. That is all that matters."

Especially, later on, I realized I needed to be with Dad whenever I could. I felt determined to be in his presence, even if just for a short visit. Every once in a while, I would see a glimmer of hope in Dad's eyes or a small improvement in his abilities. It was never anything very great, but it gave me hope. I saw God at work giving him small blessings, given his current state. While Dad suffered with dementia, facing darkness and day to day dreariness, sometimes he would make a profound statement with his actions, or acknowledge the people in the room with such openness or happiness, that at times I felt he truly loved in a childlike way. Sometimes, a simple calmness came over my father, like an acceptance of his situation, like an acceptance of God and his current life. I felt like God bestowed mercy on him. Maybe it was the medication, maybe it was acceptance, but the agitation he had earlier in his dementia seemed to be gone. He seemed content.

I would tear up as I would sing hymns to him.

One day my mother told Marcella, my daughter, "Grandpa is now on earth to love and be loved." Indeed it seemed to be true.

***

Emma, my youngest daughter, came from Arizona to visit Dad one day in the spring of 2008. She brought her son Bernie with her. He was not even a year old. I took him with me to the back porch of the home where Dad, Bernie and I sat in the shade, looking out on the sun-filled backyard. The caregiver placed a blanket over Dad to keep him warm and shelter him from the light breeze that blew that day. I handed baby Bernie to Dad and placed him in his lap so he could hold his great grandson. As Dad held him he felt the significance of the event, because he tried to smile. Dad did not smile much anymore and the muscles in his face did not work like they did at one time. It was hard to tell if the facial expression was a grimace or a smile, but based on his demeanor and based on what I knew about my father, it had to be a smile. He felt satisfied and happy.

When Emma talked to Dad, I told her to tell my father what she did for a living. She had graduated in 2006 with her teacher's certificate and Master's Degree in Education. She told him she taught physics at an Arizona High School. When I said, "You inspired her, Dad, with your teaching career." He teared up with happiness and satisfaction, but did not say a word.

Just before Christmas in November 2008, Mike and I went to visit Dad. When he stopped humming along with the songs, I knew he was not enjoying life as much. The caregivers had gotten him out of bed, placed him in his wheelchair and moved him to the living room. When we arrived "that" morning, I pulled out my guitar. We sang a few Christmas songs, and then Mike said he wanted to sing a special song for Dad. I put down my guitar and let Mike sing it a cappella. He began, like an opera singer, with his deep round throated voice.

Dad watched and listened intently.

Toward the last part of the Christmas song, Mike's voice built itself into a crescendo and he struck a high note that rattled the curtains and the paintings on the wall. Dad let out a loud joyful cry! It sounded like Dad was in pain but he was not suffering. He was enjoying the performance. It was at that moment, Mike stopped singing because he was thinking something was seriously wrong. I motioned for him to continue. Dad emotions were caught up in the sound of Mike's voice and the song he was singing. Dad must have thought about the angels, the beauty of the song he heard, the sinking to his knees and that night knowing Christ was about to be born.

As Mike finished the song, his voice trailed off and Dad sat still with tears streaming down both cheeks. Mike had sang a glorious rendition of the carol and he nailed the song; perfectly.

We both came to Dad and put our arms around

him, hugged him tightly and wept too.

FAILING MEMORY

CHAPTER 19 -- 2009

It was Tuesday, February 3, 2009. Carrie and I flew into Seattle. We were returning from a delightful mini-vacation; an extended weekend of sorts in Arizona. A couple of years prior to this date, we purchased a house with Carrie's father near Emma in Mesa, Arizona and tried to use Arizona as our vacation location as time allowed. This was especially true in the winter. At this time, I worked in Hermiston, Oregon and Seattle was a 4 hour ride from our home. It was easy to fly from Phoenix to Seattle and visit family that lived in both locations.

When I got the call from Alva, my sister, we had just arrived back in Seattle from Phoenix and had finished a visit with Carrie's family. We were leaving for Hermiston, when the phone rang. Also, at that time, Alva was visiting Mother and Dad from Riverside, California where she lived.

It was shocking news, but not unexpected, when my sister told me Dad was in the hospital with pneumonia. I told Carrie about the call and let her know that I wanted to stay near Dad. She agreed wholeheartedly. We both made arrangements with our respective employers and dashed out of the West Seattle condominium of my father-in-law's to head to Bellevue.

At some point, I anticipated receiving a call that would let me know something was seriously wrong with Dad, but I had put those thoughts out of my mind. His struggle with dementia worsened and we knew the disease itself would not cause his death, necessarily, but there may be other complications. We just did not know the form. I remained hopeful despite the fact Dad was not talking or walking, or eating and now he had pneumonia.

During that overcast day, which is typical for Seattle, I did not need to say much to Carrie. Mostly, we drove in silence to Bellevue. We traveled on I-90 over the old floating bridge south of Bellevue. Everything seemed to be a blur to me. However, I oriented myself to my surroundings. My focus was like that of a laser as I went about the task of finding the medical center.

The hospital was located right off Interstate 405, on the right hand side of the freeway; like I remembered.

FAILING MEMORY

I figured out how to exit the freeway and work my way to the hospital. We wandered around the streets trying to find the best place to park. I was rattled, when I stopped the car at a convenience store and asked a clerk for directions to the hospital entrance. The clerk told me, but I promptly forgot, except for the vague notion of "over there;" remembering she pointed her finger. Carrie and I walked briskly toward the hospital to what I thought was the entrance. We wandered, somewhat aimlessly, through the hallways until I found the guest service desk. They explained where to find the elevator.

We took the south tower elevator up to the fourth floor and asked for Dad's room number at the nurse's station. I met my siblings and Mother just outside Dad's room. My family updated me on Dad's condition and confirmed that he had pneumonia. He was lying quietly in his bed, connected to an IV and receiving a saline solution. The nurse explained to us that they had intended to stabilize Dad until he could be seen by his doctor.

Further, Alva told us, "Dad had not eaten a full meal for several days and a staff member at the adult care home called 911 to take him to the hospital." She went on, "I walked in, sat down beside his bed, and told Dad we arrived, and that we all loved him very much and wanted him to get better. I told him he was in the hospital and in a good place and will be well taken care of. I said, Larry will be here shortly."

Carrie had work in the morning and needed to head back home. Alva agreed to chauffer me around the Seattle area.

Mom said, "Your Dad is resting comfortably and is out of danger." As we waited for the doctor to arrive to provide us with her assessment, my siblings made observations about Dad that focused on how he looked, what happened upon his arrival and stated Dad was resting peacefully in the room nearby.

Then, Mom said, "Larry you should go in and see him."

I walked into the hospital room with an urgency in my step. There was the clean smell of disinfectant in contrasted to the stark and plain surroundings. I walked up to his bed and said, "Dad, I'm here. I love you and I am staying over another night." I explained that I had just returned from a trip to Arizona.

"I couldn't wait to come to the hospital just to see you."

He woke for a moment and acknowledged my presence with his eyes and made an attempt to smile. I could tell, he still felt lousy and could not or would not express it one way or another. He just laid there, mostly motionless and speechless. I grabbed his hand and sat there in silence with him for a while.

The hospital had assigned Dad a room that was located on the west side. It was a spacious unadorned room with a stiff sitting couch for guests. The couch was near to a large window, from which you could see the freeway. The beige wallpaper seemed to help create a peaceful place when you compared Dad's room to the hustle and bustle of nurses and doctors walking up and down the hallway. I saw a busy world outside Dad's hospital room.

I was struck by the stark contrast that existed in Dad's world of relative quietness and serenity and the one that functioned on the other side of his bedroom door. This included the cars on the freeway I viewed from his window.

When the geriatric doctor arrived, I excused myself saying, "Dad, I want to talk to the doctor."

My siblings, Mother and I gathered around the doctor. I asked her, "What treatment plan do you have for Dad?" We all expected him to easily kick the pneumonia and get back to living at the adult care home. We knew doctors regularly prescribed medicine that cured pneumonia and it seemed to us that Dad could simply take an antibiotic or some such pill and get better.

The doctor, somewhat defensively, explained Dad's desire was that no heroic measures be taken to save his life. At this stage of his medical condition, Dad wanted his body to travel a "natural course." The hospital had a "no added measures document" on file that Dad had signed. He did not want to be on life support of any type. Further, she explained what we already knew. Dad would probably remain immobile and continue to depend on caregivers at this aspect of his life. The documents clearly reflected what we knew, but in the moment forgot.

Many years before Dad had dementia, he made it clear to Mother that he did not want tubes stuck in him to help him cling to life without hope of ultimate recovery. At this point, Mom recalled a vivid memory of the time when she and Dad were at her cousin's, Fred's, bedside in the hospital. He had a breathing apparatus, an IV, a catheter and a feeding tube in him as he lay immobilized and restrained during his end of life illness. Dad unambiguously commented to Mother, "I DO NOT want that stuff hanging off of me when I get to that point." Dad's disgust and repulsion during that event returned to Mother. Her voice was intense when she spoke because the realization of being confronted with Dad's end of life care was daunting. Mother knew the answer. The health care instructions clearly stated Dad's expectations.

After sharing Dad's file with us, the doctor suggested hospice. She explained how hospice worked, why it was appropriate and how hospice aligned with his wishes.

I only remember the jolt that I felt and it took

several minutes for me to process the fact that my father's journey had come to an end. I was frustrated, as I thought about my father, who could receive simple care and did not have to die.

At the time, I knew my father's strong beliefs must prevail. I could hear him ask, "What kind of life would I have anyway?" My responsibility to him changed direction instantaneously and drastically. The hospital was no longer the place for him.

Immediately, the doctor recognized how devastated I was after hearing her words about Dad's condition and she empathized with me. It was not her place to offer the last word. So, she explained that we could place Dad at a convalescence center that was just down the road. They would encourage Dad to eat and give him every chance to continue his life.

The doctor observed our comportment and it sent a signal to her that we still needed a little more convincing. She started to give us more options by saying, "He looks like he is resting peacefully now and the IV is doing its job." She continued, "You could leave him here in the hospital, let him regain his strength and offer him antibiotics." That snapped me back into reality. I uttered, "No," somewhat under my breath when the doctor suggested antibiotics. It pained me to think of him continuing to live without speaking or walking as much as it pained me to put him in hospice. My siblings and Mother also had a similar reaction to mine but did not verbalize what they were thinking.

I said, "I'm convinced Dad did not want to continue to live like this." He was certainly tired of his life the way it was now and he was not going to get better. A productive life entailed communicating and being a mobile person. He did not communicate and relied on a wheelchair for mobility. We knew Dad's answer. His answer became the kindest and most generous decision that we could select.

We needed to make a final unbearable resolution; one we could not go back and change. It became a decision for him and not with him. He could not communicate with us. He did not have the problem solving abilities anymore. He took life minute by minute accepting whatever came his way.

When I composed myself, I said, "So, I guess this is it then." Alva and Mike both said, "Yes, I guess it is." Mom in her own way agreed reiterating, "I guess we have our answer." Steve was not convinced and it still bothered him that we contemplated hospice. With the exception of Steve's reluctance, I think we all felt backed into a corner and needed to honor Dad's wishes. Even Steve finally agreed.

We continued to discuss the upcoming circumstances. Should we take the doctor's recommendation of a new convalescence center or should we stick with the current adult care home? In the end, with input from the owner, we decided to return Dad to his present situation under hospice.

The owner, who was a nurse practitioner, explained to us, "We do hospice here and your father is familiar with our home and how we do things. I don't think it is a good idea for you to move him to another facility. If you're going to put him in hospice and have him live out his days in a familiar environment, keep him here." That became our final decision.

FAILING MEMORY

We planned to talk more in the morning, as we were all exhausted. For now, Dad would stay in the hospital tonight. I was not about to let Dad spend a night in an unfamiliar hospital room alone, so I decided to stay with him. When I told my family I planned to spend the night with Dad, they agreed with me and headed to their respective homes. Alva said, "I'll be back tomorrow to pick you up." I was relieved because most major decisions had been made. The hospital arranged for an ambulance to take Dad back to the adult care home the next day.

I settled in the best I could, on the hard couch, next to the window in his room with Dad in the hospital bed near me. I did not sleep much that night but gladly I spent the time listening to him breathe. The sound of his systematic but raking breath in the bed on the other side of the room was a comfort to me as I closed my eyes and tried to fall asleep. Continuously, I woke up throughout the night, stared at the moon and stars out the big hospital window or watched the big rig trucks go up and down the freeway. I listened to the roar of their engines.

Periodically, a nurse would come into the room to

check on Dad. About 10 p.m. there was a shift change. A nurse came into the room and said in a loud voice, "Heeay!" Obviously, she was good natured and this engendered a lovely way about her. Dad responded and smiled like he had always done in the past. In a cheery and as natural as could be voice he returned the greeting with, "Heeay!" Gladly, I witnessed this joyful noise that came from my father as I watched him return the greeting. It seemed he actually did feel a little better, if only for a moment. This pleased me, because the nurse had treated Dad like he was a valuable patient in the hospital. Her simple act made my father's day, because it had been the only word I had heard him utter for a complete year.

However, the joy I felt was short lived and ceased as the nurse began to work. She changed Dad, his sheets and checked his vital signs. The IV in Dad's arm twisted and turned and he winced because it must have hurt. He did not cry out in pain, but just a grimace on his face told me that he had held back a painful response. As the nurse continued to work in an efficient manner, it became obvious to me that my father viewed what she was doing as a nuisance. When she left, he lay there in silence relieved, but still groping with the aftermath of what had occurred.

The following morning, after a change in shifts, another nurse came into the room. The nurse was either told or had convinced herself that my father needed a catheter. I do not know why, but for whatever reason, she came in and said, "I am here to put a catheter in your father." I stated, "I don't think he wants one. You can try but he's not going to like it." I wish I had been more forthright and forceful because my response did not even satisfy me.

She ignored me and started preparations to put the catheter in him. I left the room. When I came back in after a few moments, she smiled and said, "He's strong. I wasn't able to put the catheter in him. He fought me all the way." As I expected.

Thinking back, I kicked myself for not being a better advocate for him by being more direct and saying, "Don't put that thing in him. He doesn't want it." It would have spared him the anguish of fighting her off.

That morning, I spent a great deal of time talking to Dad. I was trying to reassure him by talking about the plans that we had made. He was scheduled to leave the hospital today and return to his adult care home. It was the place where he had spent the last 3-4 years of his life.

I wanted to state to him that I would take him home to the bed he had spent much of his life in; at his homestead. But, I could not say that to him. There would not have been the needed, familiar caregivers and the bed that he had become accustomed to at this time. I just hoped he would understand. Yet, to this day I still keep the guilt about the end of my father's life in my mind. As Carrie often says, "You did the best for your father with the information that you had at the time and there is nothing to feel guilty about." Still, the guilty feeling persists.

Later in the morning, Alva and Mom returned to the hospital. After my call to Carrie, she also returned to Lake Forest Park. Steve and Mike said they intended to meet us at the adult care home when Dad arrived. It took forever for Dad to be discharged. He rested peacefully on his back. This was a saving grace. His hoarse breathing continued; in then out, as he scavenged for enough air. He kept his mouth open and took in all the air he could with each breath. Sometimes, he stopped breathing and my attention went straight to him, wondering if it would be his last. But, invariably, a big intake of air would occur and he would breathe out a deep breath and his raspy breathing would continue through his mouth.

The doctor arrived in the late morning and finalized Dad's discharge from the hospital. The ambulance company was notified that Dad was leaving and it took several hours before it arrived. Dad continued to rest. The nurse came in to his room and removed the IV from his arm. The paramedics arrived to transport Dad to his adult care home.

The paramedics placed Dad onto a gurney, wheeled him into the elevator and to the ambulance that was awaiting. I saw one of the paramedics aim a light down Dad's throat to assure that his breathing pathways stayed open. I was told, Dad slept through much of the transport. They planned for the worst but I was also impressed that they took great care with my father. I appreciated that level of medical care. Although, it seemed ironic in a way that they took so much care with him when we expected Dad to die naturally.

The ambulance had room for the driver and only one paramedic in the vehicle with my father. The driver and her partner readied themselves to leave for the address they were given. Alva and I prepared to leave as well. I yearned to get back to more familiar surroundings.

The winter day darkness hit me as I walked outside. Finally, Alva and I arrived at the car. We drove north toward the adult care home. We began driving by following behind the ambulance. But then, the ambulance driver took a different turn than I expected. She decided to cross the Evergreen Floating Bridge across Lake Washington into Seattle proper. You can get to Lake Forest Park going through Seattle, but it seemed like a long meandering route instead of a straightforward one. I figured they knew what they were doing or if they did not Dad would get a nice comfortable ride someplace and eventually the paramedics would find their way to his care home. Instead of continuing to drive behind the paramedics, we drove up Interstate 405 on the east side of the lake to Bothell then west to Lake Forest Park like we had done many times in the past. I knew we would beat the ambulance to the Lake Forest Park home and we did.

Once I arrived, I went inside to talk to the caregiver and let her know Dad would arrive soon. I waited for him and the ambulance for what seemed like hours, but it was just about a half hour later when the ambulance pulled up to the driveway and the paramedics wheeled him into the home. He was resting comfortably but still had the coarse rasping sound of his breathing seeking air. The caregiver lifted Dad into his bed and tucked him in for the evening. Easily, he fell back to sleep and continued his melodic breathing.

The insurance coverage included the services of a hospice social worker and nurse. They were scheduled to stop by Dad's home around 7 p.m. and talk to the family. Carrie and Mom arrived at the care home at about the same time, then later Steve, Mike and Alva joined us. We all arrived about 6:30 p.m. in preparation to meet with the hospice workers. We talked about our expectations and Carrie explained how hospice meetings normally evolve. She worked for hospice in Oregon for several years.

While we waited for the hospice workers to appear, I suggested that my siblings and I take shifts at Dad's bedside for the nighttime. I wanted a comforting face near Dad should he wake or pass during the night. We agreed that Steve would take the first shift from 9-12 a.m. since Steve normally stayed up that late anyway, Mike would watch Dad between 12-6 a.m. because he knew it would be one of the toughest shifts and I would relieve him at 6. I did not know how long we would need to continue this vigil, so I prepared myself to do my part no matter what happened.

Carrie and I had a similar experience with her mother. In 2005, Carrie's mom was in the hospital dying from cancer and her family members took turns staying in the room with her. For several days and nights Carrie's mother was not alone. I admired Carrie and her family's tenacity during that time. I wanted the same thing for my Dad. He would not be alone either.

I am very glad that my mother and siblings wholeheartedly agreed with the concept of a vigil to be with my father.

The hospice workers came at 7 p.m. and explained the process to us. They discussed the role that the family plays in making a loved one comfortable as nature takes its course. Should something happen, hospice must to be called first; not 911. Hospice is used for the person who is only expected to live 6 months or less. There are exceptions. Sometimes people rally and beat the 6 months prediction. Anything could become possible and we held onto our hopes.

Dad changed his shallow raking breathing ever so slightly and I asked his nurse what it meant. She got up, went to the bed to watch Dad for a moment and then came back to us. She said, "It sounds like the last vestiges of life. This is called chain-stoking which is a normal part of the dying process." My heart fell when I heard her words, although I expected this to occur.

The gravity of the nurse's statement hit me hard. I recall the interminable moment of silence that fell on the initial meeting the family had with hospice officials when we discussed Dad's situation.

Larry Calkins

I guess this is what they meant by *hospice*. It became real. When the meeting concluded, the nurse provided us with clear instructions for Dad's care and how we should handle everything from day to day or if necessary for months. At this point, no one expected Dad to be with us for more than a number of days. We shared contact information, gave each other hugs and said our goodbyes. The hospice workers left us with our thoughts and plans.

Alva, Mike, Carrie and Mom departed. Steve and I stayed. I wanted to give Steve some moral support for his upcoming shift. I told him I would leave around 10 p.m. I planned to walk to Mom's house and see everyone in the morning. Steve and I sat in Dad's room, quietly talking as he slept. It was important for us to stay with Dad. Gently, I held his hand and watched his breathing with my brother.

At 11:30 p.m. my younger brother Mike, returned to the adult care home. I was pleasantly surprised to see him so early. I updated Mike on Dad's condition and told him how grateful I was for his presence. I checked in with Mike to determine if he still wanted to complete his shift tonight and he assured me, "I will call you if there is any significant change in Dad's condition." He said, "Go get some rest Larry." With a grateful look in my eyes, I said "Thank you."

I said, "Let's go Steve, you can drive me to Mom's." Steve responded with his cheery, "Okay," and we left. We got back to the homestead and Steve went to his bedroom. I went to bed and tried to fall asleep with my phone nearby. I did not want to wake Mother who was in the next room slumbering away. I was keyed up and tossed and turned for a while, but then dozed off.

At 2:15 a.m., the phone rang. It was Mike. I thanked him for calling. He said Dad passed. It was February 5, 2009 at roughly 2:00 a.m. when Dad took his last breath. Mike called hospice as he had been instructed. The caregiver on staff at the adult care home called the owner. I woke Mom and Steve. I called Alva, then drove to the adult care home. We were all blurry eyed and tried to think of the instructions we had been given by the hospice workers. Slowly, we began to make arrangements through the funeral home and other contacts that were required.

I thanked Mike for being there with Dad and said, "Mike I can't tell you how much I appreciate you and I am very grateful for what you have done." I continued, "I couldn't have hoped for a better person to be with Dad at his last breath." Mike teared up and said "Dad was my hero." I said, "He was a hero to us all." Mike replied, "When Dad passed, I gave a little prayer to urge him on his way."

Dad was out of pain and no longer needed to fight his dementia. Dad, always the hero to our family did not have to suffer any longer. We believed he could fly now with the angels and he entered a much better place. Also, silently and briefly I said a prayer to the God I believed in. I asked,

"Dear God, help Dad find the pathway through the afterlife. Help him find his father and mother and find comfort in the relatives he had known as a young man and previously as a child. Also, I ask, that he be loved by the heavenly host of saints that went before and give him the peace he richly deserves."

FAILING MEMORY

All Dad's immediate family came to Dad's adult care home and the caregivers filtered in as well as the owner. I announced that Dad had passed to a better world. The men from the funeral home came in to remove him from his bed and take him to the mortuary. I said my last goodbye's to his physical body as they wheeled him out the door.

It did not stop me from thinking about him and remembering the good times I had as a child, the golf we played in Bend or the times he played with all his children and grandchildren before he passed. *Dad left a nice legacy.* I wish he could see all of his great grandchildren today. Now, I only have memories that I will share about him.

Larry Calkins

EPILOGUE – THE FUNERAL AND LEGACY

My mother, siblings and I knew Dad had shared a full life with so many people. In the end, however, his life diminished to caregivers waking him in the morning, changing him like a small child, being placed in a sling so that he could be transferred to his wheelchair with someone dressing him, brushing his teeth and hair. This was on top of him having to be wheeled to the TV for morning entertainment as he waited for breakfast and was fed his meal from a spoon and then he set in front of the TV until someone came to entertain him from the family. Then, the routine of being changed every two hours, fed lunch, more TV or whatever entertainment caregivers could provide as they cleaned the house. Then, caregivers would feed him dinner and conduct a routine that prepared him for bed. Ultimately, he did not talk, did not sing, and became totally reliant on the caregivers for his every need. His life did not have much meaning as we know it. But, from time to time I saw in his eyes and demeanor glimpses of the man I admired and loved.

Now, the relief and release occurred. Dad's relief gave way to my grief.

I spent the next few days talking to people at the funeral home making arrangements and helping Mother sign papers for Dad's final resting place. Then, I headed back home to meet my obligations at work in Oregon. Mother, my siblings and I planned a memorial service that was to be held at the Presbyterian Church where my parents worshiped on Valentine's Day, Saturday, February 14, 2009 2:00 p.m. It seemed to be the appropriate day for obvious reasons. We sent obituary announcements to the newspapers, friends and relatives telling them of Dad's passing.

To relieve my grief, I poured the next week into making memorial arrangements. I put together a slide show of Dad's life, showing joyful times and celebrations. I thought about how to stage his memorial; contemplating how to display the poignant and sublime memories I wanted to share. Therefore, I wrote a little speech to go along with the slide show. I wanted my siblings to each participate as well. I thought, the minister of the church certainly should have an appropriate sermon. I cleared all this with Mother and my siblings.

Valentine's Day came in a hurry and Carrie and I headed back to Lake Forest Park. On Friday evening, before the service, Mother offered her suggestions. My siblings and I prepared the setting for the memorial by practicing and preparing for the final curtain.

The gathering included my Dad's sister, Sarah and her family. Aunt Eva, my mother's sister, and her family were there. Also, church members, friends and family of my parents as well as my siblings attended the service. The sanctuary was full.

The service began by Mike and my Aunt Eva singing a haunting rendition of an old hymn. I first heard that song being sung a couple of years prior to this day by Dad and the daytime caregiver. He was still singing and humming tunes at that time. The caregiver would sing the first stanza and Dad would sing the second. One day, I walked in on them as they were singing together and they sounded great. I wanted to recreate that scene. I thought a rendition of the song may provide a glimpse into Dad's later stages of life at the adult care home.

Larry Calkins

After everyone came into the sanctuary and was seated, there was complete silence.

When Aunt Eva stood in the front of the congregation, she began to sing the first verse a cappella.

Then, from the back of the sanctuary, Mike began to sing the next verse.

And, Aunt Eva would counter with another verse.

Finally, Mike sung the last verse,

When they finished singing the song, Mike gave a little explanation about how Dad and his caregiver performed the hymn in the same manner with the interaction between them. This was meaningful as the words and music still rang in the ears of the congregants.

The large gathering of people listened attentively to the family as we talked about Dad and sang our way through the rest of the memorial service. The media person in the balcony showed my slide presentation of Dad's life. The pastor gave a moving account of my parent's involvement in the church. She spoke about Dad helping around the church and how kind he was to everyone.

Each one of my siblings and I gave a remembrance of my father.

Many people came to the funeral that I had not seen since childhood and when they were re-introduced to me, we had a good laugh about the early days. More importantly, I had a feeling of appreciation because so many remembered Dad affectionately.

I can say that most everyone who attended the service told stories about my father and how he touched their lives. I expressed my gratitude to them because their memories of "my Dad" reconnected me to him, relatives, friends and our community.

I knew he lived a life well executed and remembered.

A few weeks later, we placed Dad's ashes in the cemetery in Bothell, Washington. This was a much smaller gathering, of family and friends who attended the service. They told additional stories of Dad and once again confirmed that his life was well lived.

I look back on Dad's life and I cannot imagine God not being pleased with how he lived. For me, Dad's love and enjoyment of life, family as well as friends remain strong in my mind. I have lasting memories of Dad's stories about his experiences that inspires me with every step and footfall I take. I am surrounded by Dad's family, friends and acquaintances who knew the joy he spread to the world.

As mother said, "He was here to love and be loved." It is a warm and memorable farewell.

My faith and belief tell me I may one day reunite with my Dad.

ABOUT THE AUTHOR:

Larry Calkins was raised in the state of Washington. He attended a University located in Washington State. After graduation, he worked in Oregon as an Environmental Specialist. When he retired from being a state employee, Larry and his wife moved to Arizona where they currently reside.

Since retiring, Larry became interested in his family history, longed to understand his family's roots and to understand family members as individuals. This desire prompted him to write a book like this one. Other books written or published by Larry Calkins include:

To Endure – Rekindled Love; Stories of Travis Calkins
> By Larry Calkins

The Journal of Catherine Howland Bourne
> By Emma Taber Bourne

Loring Gary Calkins Senior Art Work
> A pictorial essay

Made in the USA
Las Vegas, NV
13 March 2023

69002802R00105